An Analysis of

Susan Sontag's

On Photography

Nico Epstein

Published by Macat International Ltd
24:13 Coda Centre, 189 Munster Road, London SW6 6AW.

Distributed exclusively by Routledge
2 Park Square, Milton Park, Abingdon, Oxon OX14 4RN
711 Third Avenue, New York, NY 10017, USA

Routledge is an imprint of the Taylor & Francis Group, an informa business

www.macat.com
info@macat.com

Cataloguing in Publication Data
A catalogue record for this book is available from the British Library.
Library of Congress Cataloguing-in-Publication Data is available upon request.
Cover illustration: Ross Becker

ISBN 978-1-912303-95-3 (hardback)
ISBN 978-1-912284-66-5 (paperback)
ISBN 978-1-912284-80-1 (e-book)

Notice
The information in this book is designed to orientate readers of the work under analysis,
to elucidate and contextualise its key ideas and themes, and to aid in the development
of critical thinking skills. It is not meant to be used, nor should it be used, as a
substitute for original thinking or in place of original writing or research. References and
notes are provided for informational purposes and their presence does not constitute
endorsement of the information or opinions therein. This book is presented solely for
educational purposes. It is sold on the understanding that the publisher is not engaged
to provide any scholarly advice. The publisher has made every effort to ensure that
this book is accurate and up-to-date, but makes no warranties or representations with
regard to the completeness or reliability of the information it contains. The information
and the opinions provided herein are not guaranteed or warranted to produce particular
results and may not be suitable for students of every ability. The publisher shall not be
liable for any loss, damage or disruption arising from any errors or omissions, or from
the use of this book, including, but not limited to, special, incidental, consequential or
other damages caused, or alleged to have been caused, directly or indirectly, by the
information contained within.

Printed by CPI Group (UK) Ltd, Croydon CR0 4YY

CONTENTS

THE MACAT LIBRARY

The Macat Library is a series of unique academic explorations of seminal works in the humanities and social sciences – books and papers that have had a significant and widely recognised impact on their disciplines. It has been created to serve as much more than just a summary of what lies between the covers of a great book. It illuminates and explores the influences on, ideas of, and impact of that book. Our goal is to offer a learning resource that encourages critical thinking and fosters a better, deeper understanding of important ideas.

Each publication is divided into three Sections: Influences, Ideas, and Impact. Each Section has four Modules. These explore every important facet of the work, and the responses to it.

This Section-Module structure makes a Macat Library book easy to use, but it has another important feature. Because each Macat book is written to the same format, it is possible (and encouraged!) to cross-reference multiple Macat books along the same lines of inquiry or research. This allows the reader to open up interesting interdisciplinary pathways.

To further aid your reading, lists of glossary terms and people mentioned are included at the end of this book (these are indicated by an asterisk [*] throughout) – as well as a list of works cited.

Macat has worked with the University of Cambridge to identify the elements of critical thinking and understand the ways in which six different skills combine to enable effective thinking.
Three allow us to fully understand a problem; three more give us the tools to solve it. Together, these six skills make up the **PACIER** model of critical thinking. They are:

ANALYSIS – understanding how an argument is built
EVALUATION – exploring the strengths and weaknesses of an argument
INTERPRETATION – understanding issues of meaning

CREATIVE THINKING – coming up with new ideas and fresh connections
PROBLEM-SOLVING – producing strong solutions
REASONING – creating strong arguments

To find out more, visit **WWW.MACAT.COM.**

CRITICAL THINKING AND *ON PHOTOGRAPHY*

Primary critical thinking skill: CREATIVE THINKING
Secondary critical thinking skill: INTERPRETATION

Susan Sontag's imaginative thinking in *On Photography* is part of what made her work such a breakthrough success. When presenting her arguments, Sontag creatively integrates the work of a disparate range of thinkers (photographers, authors, poets, playwrights, and film directors) to create fresh arguments about photography in contemporary culture. In doing so, she makes the case that photography is a tool used to maintain the norms of Western capitalist society.

Sontag's writing produced what, at the time, was a fresh and novel critique: an original exploration of the medium's potentialities. As an activist, she brought issues that were important to her—from across various disciplines— into focus. Writing about photography was a way for Sontag to ruminate on these interests, which included war and American consumerist culture. Her often autobiographical and polemic style of writing sought to elucidate the significance of photographic images in her life as well as in various other contexts, such as within fine art and photojournalism.

ABOUT THE AUTHOR OF THE ORIGINAL WORK

Susan Sontag was born in New York in 1933, was a celebrity icon and lauded human rights activist, cultural theorist, novelist, film director, and teacher. She is widely known for her nonfiction works: *Against Interpretation and Other Essays* (1966), *On Photography* (1977), *Illness as Metaphor* (1978) and *Regarding the Pain of Others* (2004). Her books have been translated into thirty-two languages. Among numerous rewards and accolades, she received the National Book Critics Circle Award for *On Photography* in 1978 and the Jerusalem Prize in 2001. Sontag died of cancer on December 28, 2004 in New York.

ABOUT THE AUTHOR OF THE ANALYSIS

Nico Epstein is an entrepreneur, curator, and art critic. He received his BA (Hons) at McGill University (2011) in Montreal, Canada and his MA in the History of Art with distinction at University College London (2012). Over the past six years he has organized contemporary art exhibitions and been director of the online contemporary art business ARTUNER for four years. His writing on photography has appeared at artuner.com as well as in AQNB and Photomonitor. He is currently the director of Artvisor, the contemporary art advisory platform.

ABOUT MACAT

GREAT WORKS FOR CRITICAL THINKING

Macat is focused on making the ideas of the world's great thinkers accessible and comprehensible to everybody, everywhere, in ways that promote the development of enhanced critical thinking skills.

It works with leading academics from the world's top universities to produce new analyses that focus on the ideas and the impact of the most influential works ever written across a wide variety of academic disciplines. Each of the works that sit at the heart of its growing library is an enduring example of great thinking. But by setting them in context – and looking at the influences that shaped their authors, as well as the responses they provoked – Macat encourages readers to look at these classics and game-changers with fresh eyes. Readers learn to think, engage and challenge their ideas, rather than simply accepting them.

'Macat offers an amazing first-of-its-kind tool for interdisciplinary learning and research. Its focus on works that transformed their disciplines and its rigorous approach, drawing on the world's leading experts and educational institutions, opens up a world-class education to anyone.'

Andreas Schleicher
Director for Education and Skills, Organisation for Economic
Co-operation and Development

'Macat is taking on some of the major challenges in university education ... They have drawn together a strong team of active academics who are producing teaching materials that are novel in the breadth of their approach.'

Prof Lord Broers,
former Vice-Chancellor of the University of Cambridge

'The Macat vision is exceptionally exciting. It focuses upon new modes of learning which analyse and explain seminal texts which have profoundly influenced world thinking and so social and economic development. It promotes the kind of critical thinking which is essential for any society and economy. This is the learning of the future.'

Rt Hon Charles Clarke, former UK Secretary of State for Education

'The Macat analyses provide immediate access to the critical conversation surrounding the books that have shaped their respective discipline, which will make them an invaluable resource to all of those, students and teachers, working in the field.'

Professor William Tronzo, University of California at San Diego

WAYS IN TO THE TEXT

KEY POINTS

- Marxist* and feminist* Susan Sontag (1933-2004) was a prolific and internationally acclaimed critic, theorist, and human rights activist.

- Susan Sontag's *On Photography* was an extended cross-disciplinary meditation on the medium of photography.

- *On Photography* drew attention to photography as a subject of interest and aided in the development of photographic theory.

Who Was Susan Sontag?

Susan Sontag was a twentieth century American writer who was known for her essays on modern culture. She was both a public intellectual and a pop icon. She was also a filmmaker, theatre director, and human rights activist who campaigned against war crimes and human rights abuses. She was most widely known for her non-fiction essays, and those found in *On Photography* (published in their entirety for the first time 1977) are commonly regarded as some of her best.

Susan Sontag was born 1933 in New York City. She had a difficult childhood; her often-absent mother was an alcoholic and was likely depressed, and her father died when she was five. Sontag was attractive, frequently interviewed, and never afraid to share her strong opinions. Her reputation was predicated on a series of essays which were inspired by, and extend the literary work and theories of Roland Barthes,* Walter Benjamin,* and Claude Lévi-Strauss.* Sontag established herself as a highly visible and sought after essayist in the predominantly masculine New York intellectual world of the 1960s, writing as a feminist critic for publications such as *The Partisan Review,** *The Nation,** and the *New York Review of Books,** where the essays from *On Photography* were originally published. Her writing challenged common perceptions of how we interpret art. In addition to *On Photography,* notable examples of her non-fiction writing include: *Notes on Camp* (1964), *Against Interpretation and Other Essays* (1966), *Illness as a Metaphor* (1978), and *Regarding the Pain of Others (2004).* She died of leukemia in 2004.

What Does *On Photography* Say?

Susan Sontag's *On Photography* is designed to answer several key questions: Are photographs tied in some way to reality because of the automatic way they are made? Do photographs have a special relation to reality? And, finally, can they reveal any kind of truth? Sontag's answers: photographs lack the ability to convey any knowledge, and they function as tools of capitalism* and colonialism* with capabilities of domination and submission analogous to weapons. The author describes taking photographs as a predatory tendency, an act of aggression that violates the subject of the image. According to Sontag, photographs distance us from their subjects while claiming to reveal what cannot be seen other than in a picture. These arguments are illustrated with photographs by Diane Arbus* and Edward Steichen* as well as with analyses of writings by poets such as Walt Whitman* and essayists such as Walter Benjamin.

On Photography also argues that we have an appetite for photographs which can never be satiated. We prefer images over real experience and we believe what we see in them. This is even truer today. The circulation of photographs continues to increase unabated, albeit in the form of digital images rather than the physical, printed analogue photographs that Sontag wrote about. The book is made up of essays that had previously appeared in the *New York Review of Books* between 1973 and 1977. Sontag insists that taking a photograph is analogous to attending a real-life event. This equivalency is even more pronounced today where the rapid transmission of images on social media and digitally transmitted news images give us the ability to experience events almost as they happen. In Sontag's essays, photographs inadvertently aestheticize everything they picture; they are complicit in modern day capitalism as catalysts that stimulate our desire to consume. *On Photography* earned Sontag the prestigious National Book Critics' Circle Award for Criticism in 1978.[1] It expanded her reputation beyond the New York intellectual circle to which she belonged. Delivered in the prime of her career, it remains the author's most important and recognizable collection of essays. *On Photography* helps us understand the political positions Sontag later took up and her activist tendencies. It remained a significant point of reference for the author, as indicated by her return to, and partial repudiation of, *On Photography* in *Regarding the Pain of Others* (2004) her last major publication before her death in 2004.

Why Does *On Photography* Matter?

Considered the first important book of photographic criticism, and written by one of America's most iconic intellectual figures, *On Photography* is one of the classic books on the subject. Readers engaging with it will receive an opinionated overview on the power of photographs and the ways in which we are addicted to them. It explores photography as a medium in a very broad way, merging analysis on photo-journalism with family albums and fine art photography. Photography had rarely, if ever before, been subjected to such generalizing investigation. *On Photography* represented a new means to analyze the attributes of the medium at a macro level without being tied to any specific form of photography (i.e. fine art, documentarian, etc.). Susan Sontag demonstrated that the topic was suitable for intellectual examination. Within the decade that followed its publication, critics took up and engaged with her arguments. The fields of photo history* and photo theory* became vibrant intellectual grounds, not least because of the success of her book.

On Photography is also important as a historical document. Today, Sontag's *On Photography* is not really relevant in academia except as a (somewhat dated) starting point for consideration of the problems attendant to the ever-increasing prevalence of images in our now-digital world. It is not an academic textbook, there are no footnotes and no bibliography; it is more of a meditative treatise on the subject. Outside of the classroom, photographers themselves would benefit from reading the essays in the book, as they each provide cross-disciplinary ways of considering the medium. Enthusiasts of fine art photography who aren't necessarily practitioners will in turn gain tools with which to criticize the content and subject matter of a photograph so they may articulate what has garnered their intrigue or distaste.

In a wider context, *On Photography* encourages a questioning of how we consume photographs and why we decide to take them. Although many of the examples of photographers, theorists, and critics whom Sontag references in the book are obscure and/or outdated, and are not illustrated, her broader messages are easily comprehensible to everyone with a cell phone. Lines such as, "Photographs furnish instant history, instant sociology, instant participation,"[2] remain particularly applicable to everyday life today, when the advent of global social media platforms, such as Instagram, give a new meaning to the sense of "instant" participation and history. Readers will question whether or not their trips or travel excursions are limited by the pressure to take photographs as a form of proof or documentation.

On Photography is viable as a repository and toolkit to help us unpack the meaning of photographs and to encourage us to think about their significance and power. It serves as an entrance point into photographic theory for those who have only a little background in the area. Furthermore, reading *On Photography* opens the door to broader discussions. These discussions may include: how collecting and taking photographs shapes our reality, how photographs reinforce social values, and whether or not "today," as Sontag puts it, "everything exists to end in a photograph."[3]

NOTES

1   Margalit Fox, "Susan Sontag, Social Critic With Verve, Dies at 71" *New York Times*, December 28, 2004, accessed September 28, 2017, http://www.nytimes.com/2004/12/28/books/susan-sontag-social-critic-with-verve-dies-at-71.html?mcubz=1.

2   Susan Sontag, *On Photography*, 5th edition (New York: Farrar, Straus & Giroux, 2011), 75.

3   Sontag, On Photography, 25.

SECTION 1
INFLUENCES

MODULE 1
THE AUTHOR AND THE
HISTORICAL CONTEXT

KEY POINTS

- First published as essays in the *New York Review of Books* between 1973-1977, *On Photography* was a watershed moment in photographic criticism.

- Sontag was a celebrity literary icon who wrote a lauded range of cultural criticism.

- The book was a 1970s product: photography was increasingly ubiquitous in museums, the fine art market, and US war efforts.

Why Read This Text?

Susan Sontag's *On Photography* represented an important moment in photographic criticism. Its first incarnation was as a series of essays written for the *New York Review of Books*. They were later published together as a book in 1977 in a slightly edited form. Her position outside of the photographic establishment gave Sontag the ability to use different theoretical models such as Marxism and critical theory* to address the subject in a generalist way as opposed to focusing on any one specific type of photography. This was also a cause for criticism from photographers and academics who claimed that Sontag's writing had an inherent bias and distaste for the medium. Her analysis was capacious enough to address the medium as something more than a photo in a magazine or a picture on a museum wall.

Sontag's novel exploration of the medium stems from the ways in which she questions the power of photography, our addiction to it, and its capacity to render the real. Her rhetorical prose draws together

> 66 The power of *On Photography*—is owed in part to the liberating fact that Sontag's subject was capacious enough to allow for such a free-flowing exchange with an expanding audience. In the 1970s, when Sontag was writing her essays on photography, the subject was ripe for the picking, with an appeal in equal parts high and low. 99
>
> Jed Perl, "The Middle Distance"

examples of different theorists, playwrights, critics, painters, artists and, of course, the work of specific photographers in order to illustrate that we are still living "in Plato's* Cave."* That is, we are fooled by images, confounding them with the objects they represent and taking them for reality when they are just simulations, fragments, or pieces of a larger and fluid whole.

Today, digital imagery has completely replaced analogue photography. As a result, it seems imperative that we spend more time questioning the truth claims bestowed by us upon an image. It is common knowledge that much of the photographic images we're presented with, either through news or social media, are digitally edited in one form or another. The notion of fake news—journalism intended to spread false information or hoaxes either through social media or traditional news outlets such as magazines or television—is particularly symptomatic of Sontag's conviction that we are still living in Plato's Cave. Photographs can never convey the truth.

Author's Life

Susan Sontag had a bleak, solitary, and unhappy childhood; her father died when she was just five and her mother suffered with substance absure and likely depression. Her loneliness led her to take refuge in books from an early age. She was a prodigious reader and skipped three grades in high school. By the age of 16 she was admitted to the University of Chicago where she married her professor, Philip Rieff,* within weeks of their first class together. The marriage produced a son, David Rieff,* who has managed Sontag's career posthumously, and published a variety of her diary entries and unpublished essays. After completing her Bachelor of Arts, she went on to Harvard University, where she finished a master's degree in theology. There she also began, but never completed, doctoral work, moving between different humanist studies, including theology and ethics. She also took on additional studies at Oxford University. Sontag moved to Paris in 1957, leaving behind her son and husband. Her bisexuality was fodder for the tabloids thoughout her life. Her marriage soon collapsed and, in 1959, she moved back to New York with her son.

It wasn't long before Sontag became a fixture on the predominantly male New York literary scene, writing artistic criticism for publications such as the *New York Review of Books* and the *Partisan Review.* Her affiliation with two other women also working in New York, Mary McCarthy* and Hannah Arendt,* helped further her career. "Notes on Camp" (1964) was the first essay she published in the *Partisan Review* and her first major publication of cultural criticism. It was followed by *Against Interpretation*, her earliest collection of essays, published in 1966, and the 1969 anthology of essays *Styles of Radical Will. On Photography*, which was written throughout the 1970s, aided in establishing Sontag as an internationally acclaimed critic.

Sontag would later revisit the problems that came with interpreting photographs in *Regarding the Pain of Others* (2004), the last major work of non-fiction published before her death. Here, she would abandon or contradict many of the arguments presented in her original treatise on the subject. While *On Photography* argued that photographs blanket our understanding of reality and desensitize us toward what we are looking at, *Regarding the Pain of Others* establishes their capacity to elicit compassion and their ability to bear witness by picturing emotion, two previously neglected positives.

Author's Background

The early 1970s in the United States brought nationwide student protests and increasing domestic dissatisfaction with the American military presence in Vietnam. While Susan Sontag's wide-ranging scholarly background and her stance against the American war in Vietnam* (1955-75) likely informed *On Photography*, the collection of essays is neither academic non-fiction nor a pacifist treatise. Yet, the work continuously references the predatorial nature of photography, how it is an invasive act, and how a camera is sold and advertised the same way as a weapon. "Like a car, a camera is sold as a predatory weapon ... Popular taste expects an easy, an invisible technology ... there is something predatory in the act of taking a picture. To photograph people is to violate them." [1] These views are in line with Sontag's anti-war sentiments which she sustained throughout her career. Before beginning the essays that would later make up "On Photography," she visited Hanoi. In 1968, Sontag wrote *A Trip to Hanoi* which underscored her solidarity with the Northern Vietnamese* and anti-US aggression. Mary McCarthy's *Hanoi* (1968), *The Best and Brightest* (1972) by New York Times Correspondent for the War David Halberstam, and the praised novel *Dog Soldiers* (1974) by Robert Stone were all significant texts related to the war which Sontag would have likely read while developing her ideas about photography. In Sontag's writing, photography as a tool for colonialism cannot be separated from the colonial endeavors of the United States in the Vietnam War and the way in which the camera was used there.

Additionally, at the time of writing, there was an unprecedented rise in the fine art photography market. This was supported through university courses on the medium and exhibitions of art photography in major American museums. The illustrated press was rapidly being replaced by TV broadcasts. The technologically advanced nature of easily purchasable cameras gave a previously unattainable ease of use to consumers. This image age of the 1970s inspired Sontag's extended polemic on the implications that underpin our beliefs about photography and the way photography was developing as a fine art in conjunction with painting. Similar notions were explored and expanded upon around the same time by her contemporaries John Berger* and Michael Fried* as well as by Roland Barthes.

NOTES

1   Susan Sontag, On Photography, 5th edn (New York: Farrar, Straus & Giroux, 2011), 14.

MODULE 2
ACADEMIC CONTEXT

KEY POINTS

- Although photographs had entered everyday life, their social function had not yet been critically examined.

- Michael Fried's modernist* paradigm was, at the time, a typical standpoint for reflecting on the capacity of photography.

- Marxist theory* and critical theory were beginning to enter American academia and Susan Sontag was familiar with both.

The Work in its Context

Photography was the pre-eminent vehicle for understanding world events, a most modern method of communication, and a popular amateur occupation when *On Photography* was published. The unquestioning acceptance of images and image-making was universal. As one of the most forceful components of mass media, photographs were readily acknowledged as providing an unmediated window on the world and of telling the truth. They were the norm rather than a means by which to enforce the status quo. Photography's presence in every middle-class home in the form of magazines, newspapers, advertising, and snapshots made its methods of circulation, distribution, and reception almost invisible.

At the time of Susan Sontag's writing, however, the widespread expansion of television effectively diminished the authority of the photograph as the key source of information. Photography had gained entrance into mainstream museums as art and had garnered acceptance among a growing group of collectors as a valuable commodity. Critics

> **❝** When Susan Sontag wrote about photography, photographers, or image culture in its broadest sense, even those with no special interest in these topics took notice. One of her accomplishments as a public intellectual was to make photography ... a serious subject worthy of serious critical attention. **❞**
>
> Abigail Solomon-Godeau, *Artforum*

who claimed its status as an art form did so by tying it to modernism. A critical theory articulated by Clement Greenberg,* modernism proposes that the highest form of art is one that foregrounds the particular and essential qualities of the medium which are shared by no other art form. There was no social engagement required on the part of the artist. Modernist theory applied to photography, and retroactively to nineteenth century examples, was not readily challenged by critics at the time; photography's comparability to painting as an art-form had not been formally examined. Sontag would change this. She would question the way photography operated in the mass media, in the home, and in the museum.

Indeed, *On Photography* was written at a time when photo theory was non-existent. However, the notion of photography as a slice of reality, and as an entity that possessed a fixed meaning—as Sontag describes "A photograph passe[d] for incontrovertible proof that a given thing happened"—was beginning to be challenged.[1] Meanwhile, the American war in Vietnam and the photojournalism surrounding it brought home images of the battlefield at a rapid pace. Critics questioned not only the necessity of the war, but also the significance of photographs that brought the war home and the context in which they were shown.

Overview of the Field

Michael Fried's *Art and Objecthood* (published in *Artforum* in Summer 1967) argued for the autonomy of the art object, where these objects were disconnected from the theatricality of their surroundings. This type of formalist* and Greenbergian pre-conception was typical of the Modernist standpoint that surrounded photography at the time. Fried argued that photography could exist as art form free from influence of other forms of visual art. What's more, he argued that it was representative of immediacy; that it was a medium which firmly existed in the present.

This Modernist paradigm was challenged by *On Photography*. In contrast to Fried, Sontag would argue that photography has a social function. It is something that traces reality, and that alters and mediates the way in which we perceive reality according to its context. Additionally, what it traces is not autonomous; it is something akin to Walter Benjamin's notion of the death mask.* In her words, "photography does not *simply reproduce* the real, it recycles it—a key procedure of a modern society [my emphasis]."[2] It's worth noting that Sontag's writing did not directly consider the nascent field of photographic theory and/or its underlying values. It was not a rebuke to the tenants of Modernism but an entirely new platform with which to understand the medium.

Academic Influences

The late 1960s and early 1970s witnessed the acceptance of the Frankfurt School* on the part of the New Left* (a movement in which Sontag played an important role). The New Left's incorporation of Marxism and Frankfurt School member Walter Benjamin's expanded Marxist writings were significant initiatives that played an important role in forming the academic environment in which Sontag found herself. Benjamin's assessment of photography was critical. He saw photography and film as marking a watershed in the processes of reproduction. Because they were mechanical, they brought rapid and widespread proliferation of works of art to the masses which removed their 'aura' or rarity, distance, and authenticity. Benjamin believed that photography brought a new way of seeing, one that would democratize class strictures. In 1968, Hannah Arendt edited and compiled the first English-translated anthology of Benjamin's essays, which Sontag read.[3]

In 1967, Guy Debord's* *Society of the Spectacle,* a quintessential book of Marxist critical theory and philosophy, was published. For Debord, photography was not confined by high-art theories or burdened with a historical past. Instead, it was part of what he called a spectacle: contemporary culture in which photography and other elements of mass media and popular culture mediated the social relations among people. The opening of the book foreshadows Sontag's Marxist lament on issues of representation:"The whole life of those societies in which modern conditions of production prevail presents itself as an immense accumulation of spectacles. All that once was directly lived has become mere representation."[4] Sontag was aware of Debord's concept of the spectacle and photography's role. She later cited his views in a 2002 article for *The New Yorker** that would become the basis for her book *Regarding the Pain of Others.*[5]

Lastly, Paul Wake* and Simon Malpas* make the convincing case that lines of Sontag's argument related to photography's societal function—more specifically that photographs provide a means of social control—are indebted to Michel Foucault's* *Discipline and Punish: The Birth of Prison* (1975) and his conception of panopticism.* As they describe it: "For Sontag, the power of photography derives from its ability to present itself as 'true' and unmediated whilst hiding the human intervention that 'frames' the subject."[6]

NOTES

1   Susan Sontag, *On Photography*, 5th edition (New York: Farrar, Straus & Giroux, 2011).

2   Susan Sontag, *On Photography*, 174.

3   Walter Benjamin and Hannah Arendt, *Illuminations*, trans. Harry Zohn (New York: Knopf Doubleday, 1968).

4   Guy Debord, *Society of the Spectacle* (New York: Zone Books, 1994), 1.

5   Sontag, Susan, "Looking at War: Photography's View of Devastation and Death," December 9, 2002, accessed August 10, 2017, http://www.newyorker.com/magazine/2002/12/09/looking-at-war.

6   Simon Malpas and Paul Wake, eds., *The Routledge Companion to Critical and Cultural Theory* (New York: Routledge, 2013), 298.

MODULE 3
THE PROBLEM

KEY POINTS

- Susan Sontag asks: Are photographs capable of revealing any truth and, if so, what truth do they reveal?

- The significance of photography's inclusion in museums and the way it impacted how we view photography was debated in the 1970s.

- In denying modernist tenants of photography, Sontag's text became one of the first post-modernist* critiques of the medium.

Core Question

When Susan Sontag's *On Photography* was published, critics had just begun to consider photographs worthy of attention. While most of those interested in the medium wrote about photographs as fine art and reviewed their appearances in museums and exhibitions, Sontag addressed photography's role in Western society. Her book was designed to answer this core question: Are photographs capable of revealing any truth? By addressing our experience of the image-world today—"today" being the 1970s but also the Western society of mass consumerism that began to crystallize shortly after the end of World War II (1939-1945)*—she shows that photographs lack the ability to impart knowledge and function as tools of capitalist America.

Among Sontag's peers there was a Marxist opposition to certain aspects of photography. This oppositional stance questioned not only the veracity of images, but also the common conceptualization of photography which incites our belief that we can understand, store, and/or register the entire world through images.[1] Allan Sekula*, a

> **❝** Humankind lingers unregenerately in Plato's cave,
> still reveling, it's age-old habit, in mere images of truth. **❞**
>
> Susan Sontag, *On Photography*

photographer and critic, used photography to criticize what he saw as the overarching hegemony of capitalism. A few years after the publication of Sontag's essays, Sekula would publish his most well-known essay "The Traffic in Photographs."[2] This served as a literary accompaniment to his photography wherein he discussed the medium in terms similar to those of Sontag, calling it a "capitalist world order." Like Sontag, Sekula highlighted the often overlooked corporate interests that govern forms of photographic display and, in turn, US hegemonic imperialism.[3] For example, Sekula points out that although *The Family of Man* exhibition organized by Edward Steichen at the Museum of Modern Art in 1955—which Sontag also discusses—claimed to formulate the universal experience of humanity, it was in fact employed by US companies who toured the show to further their agenda. Sontag questioned not only the way corporate entities govern the circulation of photographs in the form of fine art exhibitions and photojournalism, but also how fine art and photojournalistic displays have a flattening and all-consuming impact on our world: "[photography's] main effect is to convert the world into a department store or museum-without-walls in which every subject is depreciated into an article of consumption, promoted into an item for aesthetic appreciation."[4]

The Participants

At the time of Sontag's writing, most people understood photography as a window to the world. Photographs were distributed, for the most part, in magazines and newspapers or were made in the family and put into albums or slide shows for private consumption. Sontag wanted to understand the power of images and our attachment to them. To do this Sontag welded Marxist theory, much in the same vein as Walter Benjamin, to her notions of aesthetics. Benjamin stressed the social function of photography, a train of thought that Sontag continued.

Although photography had been accepted into mainstream museums, the implications of this, as well as questions concerning curatorial practice and organizational structures, were still being considered. While Sontag was not, strictly speaking, *against* including photography in museum collections, she questioned an acceptance based on its formal and stylistic components. Like Museum of Modern Art curator and critic John Szarkowski,* Sontag emphasized the "non-narrative nature" of photographs, while opposing his formalist stance.[4] While curators such as Szarkowski worked to establish a logical means of display for the new medium, Sontag argued that "Museums do not so much arbitrate what photographs are good or bad as offer new conditions for looking at all photographs. This procedure, which appears to be creating standards of evaluation, in fact abolishes them."[5]

Sontag was not the only writer to question the autonomous aspect of photography. Roland Barthes—whose *Camera Lucida* (1980) is, along with *On Photography,* one of the more well-known books on the subject—argues in *Mythologies* (1957) that conceiving of a photograph as an unmediated transfer of what is being captured is illusory. The photograph is part of a culturally determined system of signs. Like any other language, it is indexical.* Sontag's arguments diverge from the semiotic* approach of Barthes. She includes historical trajectories to account for the way photographic meaning has changed throughout the course of time, and the way in which Europe, America, and China differ in their understanding of, and interaction with, the medium.

The Contemporary Debate

Academic arguments surrounding the photographic medium in the 1970s revolved around a conflict between modernist and postmodernist schools of thought. Michael Fried, as a modernist critic, argued for the acceptance of photography in museums based on formal aesthetic merits and its capacity to exist outside of the social context in which it was produced. This stance was antithetical to Sontag who never separated the societal function of a photograph from the photograph itself. She argues that the inclusion of photography in museums is a "modernist victory" signaling an "open-ended definition of art [with] photography offering a much more suitable terrain than painting for this effort."[6] *On Photography* examines multiple interpretations of photography beyond it being a modern medium, and is therefore considered the "full-blown American statement of postmodernist photographic theory."[7]

Sontag did not associate herself with any of her contemporaries in her writing and did not follow the format of any one academic field. However, the debate continued about the multifaceted ways in which photography could be perceived. While Sontag didn't discuss its positives, other critics such as John Berger took a difference stance. In responding to *On Photography* in a 1978 essay, he speaks of photography's capacity for societal change in more optimistic terms: "it is just possible that photography is the prophecy of a human memory yet to be socially and politically achieved."[8]

NOTES

1 For a more in-depth account of this notion of photography in Sontag's writing, see Joan Fontcuberta and Hubertus von Amelunxen, *Photography: Crisis of History* (Barcelona: Actar, 2004), 180–1.

2 Allan Sekula "The Traffic in Photographs" *Art Journal*, Vol. 41, No. 1, Photography and the Scholar/Critic (Spring, 1981): 15-25.

3 Susan Sontag, *On Photography*, 5th edition (New York: Farrar, Straus & Giroux, 2011, 110.

4   Joel Eisinger, *Trace and Transformation: American Criticism of Photography in the Modernist Period* (Albuquerque: University of New Mexico Press, 1999), 259.

5   Sontag, *On Photography*, 141.

6   Sontag, *On Photography*, 132.

7   Eisinger, *Trace and Transformation*, 258.

8   John Berger, "Uses of Photography: For Susan Sontag," in *Understanding a Photograph,* ed. Geoff Dyer (London: Penguin, 2013), 57.

MODULE 4
THE AUTHOR'S CONTRIBUTION

KEY POINTS

- Susan Sontag aims to understand the power of images in our image-suffused world.
- The author's meditations on the medium of photography are reflective of her views on American capitalism.
- Sontag contemporized the previously established idea that photographs existed and circulated in their own world.

Author's Aims

Susan Sontag's writing in *On Photography* is polemical, autobiographical, opinionated, anachronistic, and oftentimes sends mixed messages. The book combines essays written over the span of five years, with the result that it lacks congruity and makes it difficult for readers to decipher her overall aims. There is no reason to believe that her sole desire in writing *On Photography* was to dismiss and discredit photography and the work of photographers. Rather, she wants us to question our unthinking acceptance of how photography mediates our relations with each other and with the world around us.

Sontag does a convincing job of demonstrating that photography is a way of knowing the world. Yet it is a "knowing without knowing: a way of outwitting the world, instead of making a frontal attack on it."[1] Thus, it could be argued, her key aim is to provide an extended meditation on our mistaken belief about the ontology* of the photographic image: our belief that a photograph and its subject share some magical one-to-one relationship. Sontag explains that what we gain from taking and looking at photographs is partial and fragmented. A camera can never fully capture reality itself. This is because reality,

> **❝** I got interested in writing about photography because I saw that it was this central activity that reflected all the complexities and contradictions and equivocations of this society ... *On Photography* is a case study for what it means to be living in the twentieth century in an advanced industrial consumer society. **❞**
>
> Susan Sontag, *Rolling Stone Magazine*

for Sontag, is complex and fluid; it is not facts and fragments but process and history. Ultimately, *On Photography* tells us we are deluded in our belief that the image is the physical reality of what it represents and that the content of the image is the mirror of our existence.

Approach

Despite her fame—or notoriety—in the realm of photo theory that came as a result of *On Photography*, the medium itself was a somewhat secondary interest for Sontag. She was more interested in the complexity of late-industrial capitalist society and how it was reflected in the production, dissemination, and consumption of photographs which exemplified our consumerism and commodity fetishism.* She does not examine the images commonly understood to make up photo history. Instead, she uses a wide range of examples to discuss the rapaciousness of the medium and our unfailing trust in its seeming verisimilitude.

Each of the essays in the book functions as a critical analysis in its own right. Each is self-contained and was published independently prior to its inclusion in *On Photography*. Additionally, some of the core ideas in the book had been previously visited by Sontag in other earlier publications. It could be argued that one of the claims in the eponymous first essay in *Against Interpretation* (1964)—"The earliest experience of art ... was incantatory, magical"[2] —set the stage for one

of the key arguments in *On Photography*: "the earliest *theory* of art ...
proposed that art was mimesis, imitation of reality."[3] The allegory of
Plato's Cave is also invoked in "Against Interpretation" to serve as an
example of what happens when pictures are confused with reality. Each
also concludes with a call for action. In "Against Interpretation," Sontag
argues that "In place of a hermeneutics* we need an erotics of art."[4] In
On Photography, she concludes: "If there can be a better way for the real
world to include the one of images, it will require an ecology not only
of real things but of images as well."[5]

Contribution in Context

Critics had previously commented on the uncanny* power of the
photograph. André Bazin's* 1945 essay "The Ontology of the
Photographic Image" claimed that "The photograph as such and the
object in itself share a common being, after the fashion of a fingerprint."[6]
Bazin was one of the first to draw on the affinities of Surrealism* for
photography "because it produces an image that is a reality of nature,
namely, a hallucination that is also a fact."[7]

Walter Benjamin's arguments are comparable: because photography
is a mechanical and automatic process, it brings the world directly to us
for our unquestioning consumption. It conflates any distance between
us and the thing photographed. By mechanically reproducing a work
of art thousands of miles away and bringing it into our environment, it
reduces the aura of the artwork, eradicating its rarity and power. As
Benjamin states, "that which withers in the age of mechanical
reproduction is the aura of the work of art."[8]

Benjamin, like Sontag, had also compared painting and photography,
stressing the restrictive nature of the photographic mechanism in
contrast to the more expressive and expansive capabilities of the
painter.[9] While Sontag never mentions Bazin, she makes no efforts to
conceal her admiration for Benjamin. This includes his critical interest
in film and photography. His way of writing, with its frequent use of

quotations and aphorisms, was a source of inspiration to her. He is one of the most cited writers in *On Photography* and the last chapter, an anthology of quotes, is dedicated to him.

The originality of Sontag's writing lies in its ability to combine the aforementioned sources and to position them in conjunction with contemporaneous cultural phenomena such as the American War in Vietnam and the newfound acceptance of photography into museums. Piotr A. Cieplak,* a well-regarded cultural studies* theorist, has indicated that Sontag is among the first writers on photography to include the viewer's role in the construction of the all-important relationship between reality and the still image. Indeed, she is one of the first critics to describe how social conditioning has an impact on what one sees in a photograph.[10]

NOTES

1   Susan Sontag, *On Photography*, 5th edition (New York: Farrar, Straus & Giroux, 2011), 116.

2   Susan Sontag, *Against Interpretation and Other Essays* (New York: Farrar, Strauss & Giroux, 1966), 3.

3   Sontag, *Against Interpretation*, 3.

4   Sontag, *Against Interpretation*, 7.

5   Susan Sontag, *On Photography,* 180.

6   André Bazin, "The Ontology of the Photographic Image" in *What is Cinema?, Volume 1*, translated by Hugo Gray (Oakland: University of California Press, 2005), 15.

7   Bazin, *The Ontology*, 16.

8   Walter Benjamin, "The Work of Art in the Age of Mechanical Reproduction," in *Illuminations*, trans. Harry Zohn, compiled by Hannah Arendt (New York: Knopf Doubleday, 1968), 221.

9   Walter Benjamin, "A Short History of Photography," *Screen,* Vol. 13, Issue 1, (March 1, 1972): 14.

10 Piotr A. Cieplak, "The Canon. *On Photography* by Susan Sontag," *Times Higher Education*, October 22, 2009, accessed January 10, 2013, http://www.timeshighereducation.co.uk/408739.article.

SECTION 2
IDEAS

MAIN IDEAS

KEY POINTS

- For Susan Sontag, the camera reduces all actions and subjects to aesthetic superficialities: tools of capitalist consumerism and colonial oppression.

- We remain trapped in Plato's Cave, believing images tell the truth.

- *On Photography* is a non-academic report on photography. The obscurity of Sontag's examples and the lack of illustrations make it difficult to understand.

Key Themes

Although the chapters of *On Photography* are self-contained, there are key themes that link them. One is that our familiarity with photography has had a blanketing and numbing effect on us. The omnipresent and pervasive nature of photographic images makes them incapable of representing anything other than superficial appearances. They are thus the most contemporary variation of the "usually shady commerce between art and truth."[1] They even misinform if they are without contextualization.[2] This theme is set forth throughout the first chapter, "In Plato's Cave," and is returned to enthusiastically in the conclusion. The intervening chapters, in a very broad way, actively prove this numbing effect through examples and observations of critics, writers, photographers, playwrights, and philosophers. For example, in the second chapter, Sontag describes photojournalist Walker Evans's* efforts to document the Great Depression* as an endeavor that imposes a moral uniformity: "Each thing or person photographed becomes—a photograph; and becomes, therefore, *morally* equivalent to any other of

> " Photographs are, of course, artifacts. But their
> appeal is that they also seem, in a world littered
> with photographic relics, to have the status of found
> objects—unpremeditated slices of the world. Thus,
> they trade simultaneously on the prestige of art and the
> magic of the real. "
>
> Susan Sontag, *On Photography*

his photographs.[3] The book's conclusion reinforces this sentiment: our vision has been numbed by the ubiquity of photographs. To overcome this situation, we need to come up with a "conservationist remedy," meaning we need to have an "ecology not only of real things but of images as well."[4]

As photographs obstruct truth and flatten or numb the world around us, they also reinforce the capitalist and consumerist tendencies of Western culture. Sontag's reasoning here is that Western society has become more dependent on photographs, while simultaneously becoming more detached from what they portray. We are addicted to the consumption and taking of photographic images (i.e. advertising, war journalism, travel photography), but are more and more numb to their subject matter. This addiction is not coincidental: "a capitalist society requires a culture based on images. It needs to furnish vast amounts of entertainment in order to stimulate buying and anesthetize the injuries of class, race, and sex."[5] Photographs are thus integral to the machinations of the Western capitalist system because they stimulate the desire to consume and blind us to the objects of our consumption. Meanwhile, social inequality is glazed over in the photographer's aestheticization of his/her subjects. Establishing and examining the politicized nature of *On Photography* reveals a penetrating vision that rails against American consumerist and capitalist culture.

Exploring the Ideas

To comprehend Sontag's assessment that we still confuse reality with its image, it's important to develop an understanding of the allegory that starts and closes *On Photography*. Plato was an ancient Greek philosopher of significant influence. In his Allegory of the Cave, prisoners are chained from birth to the wall of a cave. Behind the prisoners, puppets are held up to dance in front of a fire, casting shadows on the wall in front of the prisoners. The prisoners cannot see the real objects that are being moved around behind them to cast the shadows they see. Therefore, they mistake the shadows of the objects for the real thing, confusing appearance for reality. Thus, in their discussions with one another, the prisoners refer to shadows as if they were real. They know nothing else. Sontag skillfully uses this metaphor to insist that our pleasure in photography is the same as the prisoners' pleasure in the shadows. We're still inside the cave and have yet to be released into the sunlit world above where real things exist. What we see in a photograph is only a shadowy representation of the truth, not truth itself.

In exploring how photographs reinforce the power relations of Western capitalism, the American status quo, Sontag also devotes a small but significant amount of the text to images of atrocities. Ideally, such pictures should galvanize us to take action against the pain they depict, but they are not effective catalysts for social action. We are overwhelmed with a constant barrage of images. Every horrific accident or event has someone with a camera there to capture it. We find ourselves in a vicious circle where we desire the consumption of disaster photographs to confirm our distance from what is being shown. "The feeling of being exempt from calamity stimulates interest in looking at painful pictures, and looking at them suggests and strengthens the feeling that one is exempt."[6] Yet, as we continue to view images of misery we become numb. The images become more ordinary and we are less surprised as "the shock of photographed atrocities wears off with repeated viewings."[7] The author returns to this theme in more depth in *Regarding the Pain of Others,* where she concedes that photographs can bear witness and thus inspire action.

Language and Expression

On Photography is a confusing work that is not easily understandable to readers. To begin with, for a book about photography which calls upon a great number of photographers and examples of their work, it's surprising that there are no photographic illustrations. What's more, Sontag's introduction of her characters' references is scattershot. They come from a broad critical, geographical, and chronological spectrum without any logical connections. She devotes a considerable amount of text to the photography of American Diane Arbus and the writing of humanist Walt Whitman, figures relatively well known to her readers. Still, most of the other people Sontag invokes are unfamiliar; they would not have been easily recognizable for a 1970s American audience and are even less identifiable to readers today. These figures cannot be looked up easily because the book lacks an index, glossary, and bibliography. It is not an academic book. Instead, her approach is aphoristic, polemical, and journalistic.

Sontag's writing gives the impression that she is entirely negative about photography. One would be hard-pressed to find any positive assessments of the medium except for her noteworthy admission that, unlike paintings, photographs actually look better when they age: "Photographs, when they get scrofulous, tarnished, stained, cracked, faded still look good; do often look better."[8] While she hazards that photographic images could potentially be catalysts to benefit society, she sees the medium as lacking any socially redeeming qualities. The aphoristic nature of her writing consistently negates the potential for photographers to bring about social change: "Photographers … suggest the vanity of even trying to understand the world and instead propose that we collect it."[9] Practicing photography amounts to passivity on the part of both the photographer and the observer. As a human rights activist, this is a particularly problematic aspect of the medium for Sontag.

NOTES

1   Susan Sontag, *On Photography*, 5th edition (New York: Farrar, Straus & Giroux, 2011), 11.

2   Sontag, *On Photography*, 4.

3   Sontag, *On Photography*, 31.

4   Sontag, *On Photography*, 180.

5   Sontag, *On Photography*, 178.

6   Sontag, *On Photography*, 168.

7   Sontag, *On Photography*, 20.

8   Sontag, *On Photography*, 79.

9   Sontag, *On Photography*, 82.

MODULE 6
SECONDARY IDEAS

KEY POINTS

- Reflecting on photography as a capitalist instrument of coercion involves consideration of how it is both an art form and a weapon.
- For Susan Sontag, when it comes to discussing the mediums of fine art, photography is of lower value than painting.
- Sontag's conceptualization of the artistry involved in photojournalism has been overlooked.

Other Ideas

Photography, for Susan Sontag, is a tool that serves the power relations of the capitalist democracy in which we live. It serves as a means by which the ideology of capitalism is perpetuated and disseminated. Accordingly, for the author, it is of no aesthetic merit. Nonetheless, Sontag devotes a considerable amount of text to a discussion of how photography functions as an art form. Her tone is mostly critical. She argues, "though some photographs, considered as individual objects, have the bite and sweet gravity of important works of art, the proliferation of photographs is ultimately an affirmation of kitsch."[1] The ways in which photography can be called art are different from the ways in which painting can be called art. The distinction, but also the reciprocity between the two, is of importance to Sontag.

Sontag aligns the act of picture taking with the act of discharging a weapon and, more largely, with colonizing efforts in the United States. She describes photography in the latter half of nineteenth century

> **❝** By the power of photography, the natural image of a world that we neither know nor can know, nature at last does more than imitate art: she imitates the artist. **❞**
>
> André Bazin, *The Ontology of the Photographic Image*

America as something that came hand in hand with the subjugation and suppression of Native peoples. Early settlers photographed natives to instill the perception that they were inferior to the white populace which, in turn, supplied a justification for war and taking over their land. In chapter 2, "Melancholy Objects," she illustrates this "colonization through photography" with the photographs of A.C. Vroman.[*2] His ability to get indigenous Americans to pose for him was an example of "the predatory side of photography ... evident earlier in the United States than anywhere else."[3] Despite the belligerent behavior that the author claims comes with the act of using a camera, Sontag also concedes that the impact of a photograph might be contingent on its contextualization. "A photograph that brings news of some unsuspected zone of misery cannot make a dent in public opinion unless there is an appropriate context of feeling and attitude."[4]

Exploring the Ideas

According to the author, the way in which paintings are organized, archived, and displayed in the context of a fine art museum is distinct from how fine art photographs are categorized in the same setting. While paintings have the potential to belong to an established canon,[*] that is, art works that have been validated as influential and significant, "the museum cannot be said to have created a secure canon for the photographic work of the past, as it has for painting."[5] The inclusion of photography in the museum doesn't create standards of evaluation in the same ways it does for painting. In fact, it abolishes them.[6]

Sontag places a higher value on paintings than she does photography. "[A] painting is commissioned or bought," she writes, "[while] a photograph is found (in albums or drawers), cut out (of newspapers and magazines), or easily taken oneself."[7] This is less true today when contemporary art is synonymous with photography. Top-end photographers are now commissioned for portraits and photography prices are the equivalent of paintings, or more.

Sontag insists that the camera is used as a weapon, specifically a weapon of American capitalism, colonization, and tourism. We "load" the film of a camera, we "aim" the camera to focus on our "targets" and we "shoot" to capture the image. The author indicates that cameras are sold using the same lexicon as rifles. To prove her point, Sontag quotes from an ad for an analogue camera, the Yashica Electro-35 GT: "Take beautiful pictures day or night. Automatically. Without any nonsense. Just aim, focus and shoot. The GT's computer brain and electronic shutter will do the rest."[8] In *On Photography*, Sontag makes the case that cameras are not only used in war, they're also marketed to us in the same way as weapons.

Overlooked

Sontag's perceptive analysis of how a photojournalist takes pictures is not often discussed by photo theorists today. Nonetheless, it marks an important starting point for the development of a topic she returned to in more depth in *Regarding the Pain of Others*. Much of *On Photography* stresses the normalizing effect that photographic images have on their viewers. She describes it as a form of leveling that makes things appear equal. For the work of photojournalists, the same is true. We value uniformity; we value an approach that presents the situation as being as true to life as possible: "the very success of photojournalism lies in the difficulty of distinguishing one superior photographer's work from another's, except insofar as he or she has monopolized a particular subject."[9] The variable for success is the photojournalist's lack of presence, his or her ability *not* to be there when he or she takes the photograph. This represents a form of artistry in and of itself.

The act of taking a photograph, especially a war photograph, which is one of Sontag's most commonly used examples, is thus an anti-interventionist act, an act of compliance. The logical next question is: what would a social or civic engagement look like between the photojournalist and his or her subject? Using Sontag's arguments as a starting point for a broader discussion on the topic, photo theorist Ariella Azoulay* re-engaged with Sontag's stance, devoting an entire book to arguing that photojournalists have now become civically engaged with those they photograph through the lens of their cameras.[10]

Though in the 1970s photojournalist images had just begun to enter contemporary art venues, the artist press photographer is someone who has now been fully institutionalized within the fine art museum. Works by contemporary photographers whose practice is rooted in photojournalism, such as Sebastião Salgado* and Luc Delahaye,* can be readily found in museums and galleries precisely because of their mastery over the techniques Sontag outlines.

NOTES

1 Susan Sontag, *On Photography*, 5th edition (New York: Farrar, Straus & Giroux, 2011), 81.

2 Sontag, *On Photography*, 50.

3 Sontag, *On Photography*, 64.

4 Sontag, *On Photography*, 17.

5 Sontag, *On Photography*, 141.

6 Sontag, *On Photography*, 141.

7 Sontag, *On Photography*, 79.

8 Sontag, *On Photography*, 14.

9 Sontag, *On Photography*, 133.

10 See Ariella Azulay, *The Civil Contract of Photography* (Cambridge, MA: MIT Press, 2008).

MODULE 7
ACHIEVEMENT

KEY POINTS

- *On Photography* galvanized the photographic community.

- It became a source of inspiration for others conscious of the medium's inroads into museums.

- The advent of digital images makes Susan Sontag's fear of an image-flooded world visionary.

Assessing the Argument

On Photography succeeds in being profoundly skeptical about the medium. It is pessimistic about the potential benefits of photographs either as instruments of social change or as fine art. As a result, the publication brought a strong response from photographers and from academics who had begun to study the medium. It opened new ways of examining photography, proving that the medium was fertile ground for exploration.

Indeed, *On Photography* was one of the first books to support photography as an object of critical inquiry and to question its role in society. It consequently spawned a raft of critical writing. For example, Allan Sekula expanded Susan Sontag's investigation of the role of photography in power relations. Nevertheless, today, as the art critic Jed Perl* points out, Sontag's "skepticism has given the book a somewhat questionable role in scholarly circles."[1] This is perhaps because of the stream of consciousness tonality that Sontag uses to present the subject matter. Her prose is aphoristic and reflects her pre-occupations with American hegemony which come from her position as a 1970s feminist and human rights activist. It could be said that her lack of specialty in the field of photography allowed her to analyze it

> ❝ Sontag's claims about photography, as well as her mode of argument, have become part of the rhetorical 'tool kit' that photography theorists and critics carry around in their heads. ❞
>
> Michael Starenko, "Sontag's Reception," *Afterimage*

in so many ways and set the groundwork for an expansion of photo theory in American Academia.

Achievement in Context

Sontag's assessment of photography was successful in denying the medium any form of ethical agency, especially in the context of the American military aggression in Vietnam. The author's apparent anti-Vietnam war and anti-colonialist sentiments in her discussion of the medium appealed to a segment of the reading public who shared her views. Nevertheless, it's worth noting that, by the time Sontag began her investigation in 1972, television had replaced photography as the key witness to the war. Still images may have affected her more deeply than they did the general American populace. This would have made her assessments of war photography less understandable to the general public at the time.

Sontag's autobiographical manner of writing was also one of the reasons for the book's success. The arguments themselves are primarily pyrotechnics of rhetoric which add a degree of confusion when scrutinized. However, because of Sontag's public persona and position as a celebrity intellectual, when she chose to speak about photography she already had the ear of a wide segment of the American public. As the essays which make up each of the chapters of *On Photography* were published sequentially in the popular *New York Review of Books,* Sontag was able to build momentum and intrigue from her readership before the final version of the book was published in 1977.

Limitations

In the academic discipline of political science,* *On Photography* has been used to analyze notions of responsible citizenship. International affairs* expert David Campbell,* for example, analyzes the politics, ethics, and importance of the way we consume images of modern warfare.[2] Regarding the 2003 invasion of Iraq,* Campbell adopts Sontag's perception that manufacturing images of atrocity makes the photographers accomplices in contemporary conflicts. He concludes that the "relatively bloodless coverage" of the invasion makes the media out to be accomplices who "share the responsibility for glamorizing coverage of war."[3] The application of ideas expressed in *On Photography* in the realms of political science and politics were also fostered by Sontag's own work in Sarajevo (1993–96) during the Yugoslavian Civil War (1991-2001).* There she withstood gunfire to author and stage a play while promoting humanitarian rights in conjunction with her writing.[4]

As academics in the late 1970s seized on the theories of Jacques Derrida* and Michel Foucault to demonstrate that images were not innocent or neutral but instead were pawns in the legitimization of power relations in late capitalist society, new methodologies to understand their significance were introduced. The application of theories of semiotics,* structuralism,* psychoanalysis,* Marxism, and feminism* were applied to photographic studies in academia. With this shift, Sontag's lack of academic rigor became more apparent and her views were both expanded and superseded.

Rather than being attacked, *On Photography* faded from influence as its arguments were expanded upon by the subsequent generation of scholars. The field of visual studies* arose in the 1990s to place photography within a wider history of image-making practices. Photography's function in a specific context—for example, the construction of race, gender, or colonization—became the focus. The text, however, remains relevant both historically as a pioneering work, and as a work of prophecy in its description of the ways we understand and try to deal with the plethora of images in the digital world.

NOTES

1   Jed Perl, "The Middle Distance," *New Republic*, May 4, 2012, accessed December 12, 2012, http://www.newrepublic.com/article/books-and-arts/magazine/103068/susan-sontag-journals-notebooks-consciousness-harnessed-flesh.

2   See David Campbell, "Representing Contemporary War," *Ethics and International Affairs* 17, no. 2 (2003).

3   David Campbell, "Cultural Governance and Pictorial Resistance: Reflections on the Imaging of War," *Review of International Studies* 29, no. 1 (2003): 57–73.

4   For her own description of her role there, see Susan Sontag, "Waiting for Godot in Sarajevo," *Performing Arts Journal* 16, no. 2 (1994).

MODULE 8
PLACE IN THE AUTHOR'S WORK

KEY POINTS

- Two photographs of concentration camps* had a profound impact on the author; her interest was part of her drive to uncover truth.

- Susan Sontag's career was cross-disciplinary and devoted to challenging injustice with her own brand of human rights activism.

- *On Photography* picks up Sontag's earlier ideas on the excesses of American culture, which she would return to later in her career.

Positioning

Susan Sontag has claimed that her interest in the aesthetic and moral aspects of photography began when she encountered photographs of the Bergen-Belsen* and Dachau* concentration camps in 1945 when she was 12. The author describes the poignant encounter in the first chapter of the book: "Nothing I have seen—in photographs or in real life—ever cut me as sharply, deeply, instantaneously. Indeed, it seems plausible to me to divide my life into two parts, before I saw those photographs and after."[1] *On Photography* was Sontag's way of working through this traumatizing experience, her attempt, in the words of art historian Jae Emerling* "to grapple with these images by addressing their aesthetic existence."[2]

Much of Sontag's previous career as a writer and public intellectual was devoted to how, and if, art of any kind has the capacity to render truth, and how this truth can be discerned. Her essay "Against Interpretation" (1964) began this particular line of enquiry. In it,

> ❝ It all started with one essay — about some of the problems, aesthetic and moral, posed by the omnipresence of photographed images; but the more I thought about what photographs are, the more complex and suggestive they became. So one generated another, and that one (to my bemusement) another, and so on — a progress of essays … ❞
>
> Susan Sontag, *On Photography* (preface)

Sontag opposed the sort of interpretation that replaces art with a fixed statement of meaning as this is what makes its truth value indeterminable. It is also in "Against Interpretation" that Sontag decries the excess of American culture which leads to a "steady loss of sharpness in our sensory faculties."[3] Photography's numbing effects are a product of the overproduction of images. In *Regarding the Pain of Others,* Sontag reconsiders these effects to suggest that photographs can bear witness.

Photography was thus an enduring theme in her writing throughout Sontag's intellectual life and is tied into her overarching interest in uncovering how artworks render truth.

Integration

Susan Sontag was a novelist, filmmaker, and critic, not a scholar. She had no ties to academia. As public intellectual, she introduced notions of power relations adopted from French theorists such as Michel Foucault, Jacques Derrida, and Guy Debord. These concepts subsequently came to permeate academia in the Anglo-Saxon world. She wrote *On Photography*, the essays "Against Interpretation" and "Notes on Camp," and the book *Illness as a Metaphor* during a period in her career in which she produced her most important, influential, and praised non-fiction work (1964-1980). This was a time in which she came into her own as a writer.[4] As a testament to the significance of the book, *On Photography* spawned a TV series, *It's Stolen Your Face*, which was based on the essays. Sontag hosted the series, which was shown on the British Broadcasting Corporation (BBC)* in 1978.

Although Sontag's corpus is wide ranging, there is a common thread: speaking out on behalf of human rights at a tumultuous period in twentieth century history. Her criticism and literary work concentrates on the importance of feminism, ethical citizenship,* and fighting injustice. Though *On Photography* is not a pacifist treatise, it is informed by her stance against the American War in Vietnam which is referenced throughout the work most often as a way to describe the negative effects of photography.

Significance

Sontag's non-fiction writing has appealed to many different audiences. Much of her film criticism is still used today in universities. Her "Notes on Camp" is the first attempt to define a gay sensibility. "Against Interpretation" and its famous rallying cry for "an erotics of art" was an inspiration for 1970s "gonzo journalism,"* a writing style that amalgamates literature and reportage while melding fact and fiction.[5]

On Photography launched careers in photographic criticism, supported the academic inroads of French theory,* and made photography a suitable object of intellectual investigation. With the enormous expansion of digital images, Sontag's fears about the medium are still prescient today. For those who study photography, it remains her most famous work.

Sontag's ideas were articulated rhetorically and were not scholarly enough to be disproved. The power of that rhetoric, however, was inspirational. She can be seen as a pioneer in what we now call visual studies, an academic discipline which emerged in the 1990s. Denying that the photograph is an unmediated image of the real, like Sontag does, visual studies describes photographs as just one kind of image. It also recognizes them as part of a larger system whose use depends on the context and discourse in which they circulate, whether it be advertising, fashion, war, or art.

Sontag's private life was persistently intertwined with her writing. Her *Illness as Metaphor* (1978) was written after she experienced a bout of breast cancer. Bisexual and part of the gay community in New York, she considered the AIDS crisis in *Aids and its Metaphors* (1989), later writing a play about it, *The Way We Live Now* (1990). Never hesitating to speak out, Sontag was the object of media attention throughout her life. Indeed, her reputation could be said to be based on her life; she was a celebrity, politically active, and often interviewed. She was outspoken and a cultural icon. Since her death, her name has remained prominent, not only for her writing and films but also for her intimate relationship with celebrity photographer Annie Leibowitz.

NOTES

1   Susan Sontag, *On Photography*, 5th edition (New York: Farrar, Straus & Giroux, 2011), 20.

2   Jae Emerling, *Photography History and Theory*, London and New York City: Routledge, 2012, 114.

3   Susan Sontag "Against Interpretation," Against Interpretation and Other Essays. New York: Farrar, Strauss & Giroux. 1963: 13

4   Emily Greenhouse, "Can We Ever Know Sontag?," *New Yorker Blog*, accessed December 19, 2012, http://www.newyorker.com/online/blogs/books/2012/04/can-we-ever-know-sontag.html. See also Susan Sontag and David Rieff, *As Consciousness is Harnessed to Flesh: Journals and Notebooks, 1964–1980* (New York: Farrar, Straus & Giroux, 2012).

5   Sontag "Against Interpretation," 7.

SECTION 3
IMPACT

THE FIRST RESPONSES

KEY POINTS

- Critics from the photographic community were predominantly hostile as they saw the book as an attack on the medium.
- Susan Sontag made little effort to defend herself against these attacks.
- However, Sontag would reverse a core argument offered by *On Photography* in a later publication.

Criticism

Critics who were part of the American photographic establishment were mostly hostile to *On Photography* when it first came out. One common refrain from these individuals was that Susan Sontag had a distaste for a medium with which she had no familiarity since she was not a practitioner. According to photographer and critic Michael Lesy,* "There is no evidence in the book that its author has ever used a still camera, engaged in research in a photographic archive, or interviewed any practitioners of the medium."[1] Lesy believed Sontag was speaking autobiographically and in defamatory terms about photographs of which she knew nothing. It was uncommon to see critics who wrote in photographic magazines offer any form of praise after the book's initial publication. Instead, reviews in these specialized publications were more often used to defend photography from what the writers saw as Sontag's unfounded attacks on the medium.

However, there were some members of the photographic community who felt that the book had a positive impact. Photo critic

> ❝ The initial critical reception of Susan Sontag's *On Photography* (1977) is one of the most extraordinary events in the history of photography and cultural criticism. No other photography book [had] received a wider range of press coverage than *On Photography*. ❞
>
> Michael Starenko, "Sontag's Reception," *Afterimage.*

David Levi Strauss* has mused that while many of his peers reacted with animosity, "for [him], *On Photography*, opened the field, and made it all active, again."[2] Some saw it as a catalyst that expanded the way photography could be written about. Others even saw it as a necessary confrontation with the medium that flagged significant problems with photography. As critic and historian John McCole* wrote in 1979, "the issues she raises will have to be faced, not only by radical critics, but by anyone who thinks and cares about photography."[3]

Responses

Since the original form of *On Photography* came as six sequential and self-contained essays published in the *New York Review of Books*, Sontag responded to criticism before the completed work was published as a book. These responses came at different symposia and panels to which she was invited, and in intellectual exchanges in other publications during the period.

Sontag readily admitted to being an outsider and identified as such. As she proclaimed in a 1975 speech at Wellesley College: "I am above all not a critic of photography. But it's from that strictly independent and freelance position that I am saying my say; it's not as a member of the photography establishment or photography anti-establishment, but as an educated outsider."[4] Thus, criticism from members of the photographic establishment ultimately had little effect on Sontag since she had never claimed to be a photo-critic or expert in the field of photography. In the author's view, being a non-specialist gave her the capability to provide a more well-rounded perspective.

Sontag did not opt to directly defend herself by confronting her detractors with personal attacks. Instead, she suggested *On Photography* was an undertaking that reflected her views about society at large. As she described in a 1982 discussion with American author and interviewer Charles Ruas* in the *New York Times*: "*On Photography* is a complicated account … ultimately it's about the modern world, about consumerist consciousness, about capitalism; it's about all sorts of moral and esthetic attitudes that photography seems the most extraordinary and rich example of."[5]

Conflict and Consensus

Over time, the grievances that the American photographic establishment has had with *On Photography* have diminished. In the immediate years after publication, excerpts and sections of the book were republished in major anthologies of photographic history and theory.[6] During the 1980s, however, such reprints waned. Sontag's critique of photography was overshadowed as art critics and theorists like Douglas Crimp*, Abigail Solomon-Godeau,* Allan Sekula, and Rosalind Krauss* protested the way in which the art-historical establishment co-opted photography as art. Though they did not cite *On Photography* directly, their writing depended on Sontag's work as they analyzed the conditions through which authority and meaning is bestowed upon a photographic image. Their application of a variety of theoretical perspectives, including Marxism, feminism, and semiotics, made the medium central to postmodernist criticism and made earlier forms of critique, such as Sontag's, less relevant in the context of American academia.

One of Sontag's core arguments was that photographs had an anesthetizing effect, that they numbed us to the plight of the world.

However, she would later reverse her opinion when describing photographs of disasters and atrocities in *Regarding the Pain of Others* in 2003. There, she questioned her own view that photographs could not communicate suffering or elicit compassion. She describes this reversal of opinion as follows: "I wrote [in *On Photography*, that] photographs shrivel sympathy. Is this true? I thought it was when I wrote it. I'm not so sure now. What is the evidence that photographs have a diminishing impact, that our culture of spectacle neutralizes the moral force of photographs of atrocities?"[7]

NOTES

1   Michael Lesy, "An Unacknowledged Autobiography," *Afterimage* 5, no. 7 (January 1978): 5.

2   Katy Siegel (Quoting David Levi Strauss), "On Susan Sontag (1933–2004)," *The Brooklyn Rail*, February 1, 2005, accessed December 15, 2012, http://brooklynrail.org/2005/02/art/on-susan-sontag-1933-2004.

3   John McCole. "Walter Benjamin, Susan Sontag, and the Radical Critique of Photography," Afterimage Vol. 7 No.1–2 (Summer 1979): 14.

4   The ASX Team, "Susan Sontag: Speech and Interview at Wellesley College" *American Suburb X*, June 11, 2013, accessed August 18, 2017, http://www.americansuburbx.com/2013/06/susan-sontag-speech-and-inteview-at-wellesley-college-1975.html.

5   Charles Ruas, "Susan Sontag: Pas, Present and Future" *The New York Times*, October 24, 1982, accessed August 15, 2017, http://www.nytimes.com/books/00/03/12/specials/sontag-past.html?mcubz=1.

6   See for example, Vicki Goldberg, *Photography in Print: Writings from 1816 to the Present* (Albuquerque: University of New Mexico Press, 1981).

7   Susan Sontag, *Regarding the Pain of Others* (New York: Picador, 2004): 82.

MODULE 10
THE EVOLVING DEBATE

KEY POINTS

- Susan Sontag's insistence that our experience of the world is governed by pictures was taken up by post-modernist critics.

- Her belief that photographs of dreadful events could not encourage empathy was expanded upon by affect theorists.

- In the current academic discourse surrounding photographic theory and criticism, *On Photography* is not often cited or referenced.

Uses and Problems

Within five years of the book's publication, the field of photographic theory became a vibrant intellectual area. While Susan Sontag's writing did not play a big part, it was an example to be followed in academia. Sontag had demonstrated that photography was a medium worthy of enquiry and critique, and not an inert technology.

Rosalind Krauss, one of the founders and editors of the highly influential art magazine *October*,* re-visited Sontag's question of whether photography was art. Her significant essay, "Photography's Discursive Spaces: Landscape/View", published in the *Art Journal* in 1982, claimed that photographs originally intended for the archive and placed on gallery walls falsified photographic history.[1] Douglas Crimp, Krauss's colleague at *October*, railed against photography as Sontag did: "Next to these pictures, firsthand experience begins to retreat, to seem more and more trivial. While it once seemed that pictures had the function of interpreting reality, it now seems that they

> **❝** Flooded with images of the sort that once used
> to shock and arouse indignation, we are losing our
> capacity to react ... So runs the familiar diagnosis. But
> what is really being asked for here? ... that we work
> toward an "ecology of images," as I suggested in *On
> Photography* ? But there *isn't* going to be an ecology of
> images. **❞**
>
> Susan Sontag, "Looking at War"

have usurped it."[2] *On Photography's* consideration of photography as aggressive cultural tourism in which photographers are passive and not engaged with their subjects was used by critic and artist Martha Rosler* in her critique of contemporary documentary practice "In, Around and Afterthoughts (On Documentary Photography)" (1981) and in her own art. Similarly, Allan Sekula took up Sontag's inquiry into the politics of representation in a number of seminal essays published in 1984 as *Photography Against the Grain*.[3] Sontag revisited her own ideas about photographic depictions of pain, suffering, disasters, and atrocities in *Regarding the Pain of Others*, and again in "Regarding the Torture of Others" (2004), an essay on the photographs of torture at Abu Ghraib.*[4] As with all the other aspects of photography she wrote about, such images became the center of a larger debate involving the notion of affect theory.*

On Photography also deals with the cruelty of a camera, a device Sontag claims violates its subjects. To photograph people is also "necessarily 'cruel' [and] the camera is a kind of passport that annihilates moral boundaries."[5] Susie Linfield's* *The Cruel Radiance* (2011) discusses this cruelty in more depth. The photography theorist credits Sontag and *On Photography* throughout, going so far as to call her style of writing a "Sontagian approach."[6] Essentially, Linfield re-evaluates the notion of the witness in the face of cruel images while stressing the continued relevance of photojournalism. Linfield's writing is typical of the school of photographic criticism today known as affect theory, which continues to rediscover uses for *On Photography*.

Schools of Thought

Sontag inspired the photo critics who were most prominent during the 1980s. While these critics did not cite or mention Sontag directly, their arguments, which are polemic in tone and in context, echo those of Sontag.[7] Today, the now-undisputed acceptance of photography in mainstream art institutions like museums and galleries, signifies—to these critics—the triumph of the market for photographs over photographic meaning. There is a degree of irony to this. After the publishing of her most well-regarded neo-Marxist* texts in the 1970s and 80s, Martha Rosler's career as an artist continued to bloom, elevating her toward the apex of the contemporary art market. Artists such as Rosler, and to a lesser extent Sekula, who criticized the way in which photographs circulated have also, to a certain degree, depended on the relevance of the medium as an art form—not to mention its market—in order to support their careers.

With regards to examining the affective nature of photographs, Susie Linfield maintains that *On Photography*'s claims concerning the witnessing of atrocity ("the shock of photographed atrocities wears off with repeated viewings … the vast photographic catalogue of misery and injustice throughout the world has given everyone a certain familiarity with atrocity") are more impactful than the later claims of *Regarding the Pain of Others*, which stress the potential for a compassionate response from viewers of photographs of atrocity.[8] In essence, Sontag's sentiment informs all of Linfield's *Cruel Radiance*, which questions the motivations we have in looking at images of atrocity and the implications of this affected observation.

In Current Scholarship

On Photography's place in current scholarship is limited. It is not often included in new anthologies of photo theory or photo-criticism which is an important marker of contemporaneity and/or gravitas in academia. Writing on the reception of *On Photography* in the well-regarded photography journal *Afterimage*, American critic Michael Starenko* offers a cogent assessment of the book's place in current academic discourse. He claims that in the years since its publication, "photography theory and criticism has developed into an academic sub-discipline that has little if any strategic use for *On Photography*. The product of a sensibility rather than a research methodology, and written by a public intellectual ... *On Photography* cannot be used to advance either the field or professional careers."[9] This has not changed since the appearance of Starenko's article, written in 1998 on the 20-year anniversary of the book's publication, and "explains why *On Photography* is alluded to, but not directly cited by contemporary academics."[11]

Currently, David Rieff, Sontag's only son, continues to develop the ideas espoused in *On Photography* through his directorship of the Susan Sontag Foundation.* The foundation was created to honor and promote "talented emerging artists in a variety of disciplines [and] the international exchange of language and culture."[12] The foundation endorses Sontag as a literary figure, and helps to preserve her legacy as a champion of art, an original thinker, and a critic. Rieff continues to publish his mother's writing. This came most recently in the form of her collected journals, *As Consciousness Is Harnessed to Flesh: Journals and Notebooks, 1964-1980*, published in 2012. Since Sontag had sold her literary archive and its accompanying rights to an American university, UCLA,* they may have been published regardless of Rieff's involvement. Rieff has nevertheless chosen to aid in developing the public's understanding of Sontag's writing. *As Consciousness* provides contextualization for scholars interested in learning more about the environment and writing process that were part of *On Photography*.

NOTES

1   Rosalind Krauss, "Photography's Discursive Spaces: Landscape/View," *Art Journal* 42, no. 2 (1982), 311-319.

2   Douglas Crimp, *Pictures* (New York: Artists Space; Committee for the Visual Arts, 1977), 3.

3   Alan Sekula, *Photography Against the Grain* (Halifax: Press of the Nova Scotia College of Art and Design, 1984).

4   Susan Sontag, "Regarding the Torture of Others," *The New York Times Magazine*, May 23, 2004, accessed August 19, 2017, http://www.nytimes.com/2004/05/23/magazine/regarding-the-torture-of-others.html?_r=0.

5   Susan Sontag, *On Photography*, 5th edition (New York: Farrar, Straus & Giroux, 2011), 41

6   Susie Linfield, *The Cruel Radiance: Photography and Political Violence* (Chicago: University of Chicago Press), 156.

7   For further details on this, see See Michael Starenko, "Sontag's Reception," *Afterimage* 25, no. 5 (1998).

8   Linfield, *The Cruel Radiance*, 7; 262–3 (quoting pages 20–1 of Sontag's On Photography).

9   Michael Starenko, "Sontag's Reception," 6.

10   Michael Starenko, "Sontag's Reception," 6.

11   For further information on the Susan Sontag Foundation, visit the website http://www.susansontag.com.

12   The Associated Press, "Sontag Sells her Papers to U.C.L.A," The New York Times, January 17, 2002, accessed August 20, 2017 http://www.nytimes.com/2002/01/27/us/sontag-sells-her-papers-to-ucla.html?mcubz=1.

MODULE 11
IMPACT AND INFLUENCE TODAY

KEY POINTS

- *On Photography* serves as an example of rhetorical flourish. It has had little impact in academic circles.

- We interact with photography very differently than Sontag did in the 1970s; accordingly, her book is seldom referenced by academics.

- Political scientists today discuss the results of photojournalism, an activity Sontag had described as having few positive attributes.

Position

On Photography is a historical starting point for considering the problems attendant to the ever-increasing prevalence of images in our now-digital world. It is provocative as a state of mind to reference or as a mental toolkit, but not as a scholarly resource.[1] Its issues are considered by academics in a broader sense, but the work is not often cited or quoted specifically in contemporary scholarship. Core themes of the book— our belief in the transparent nature of the medium, the importance of acknowledging the power of the photograph, and the fact that we live in a world saturated by images which we have little control over—have been absorbed by visual culture studies. However, the book itself is rarely taught in a university classroom related to that discipline.

Sontag's *Regarding the Pain of Others* has also reduced the power of the opinions she expressed so firmly in *On Photography*. Here, Sontag ended up re-engaging with war photojournalism and, in the words of theorist Sohnya Sayres* offered "a palinode to some of her harsh pronouncements about the limits of photography in the ethical realm

> 66 [Sontag's] solution was to call for 'an ecology of
> images,' and it is hard to think of an appeal that has gone
> more spectacularly unheeded. 99
>
> A. O. Scott, "On (Digital) Photography: Sontag, 34 Years Later"

[despite maintaining] a certain skepticism about images" from so-called conscious photographers.[2] Sontag explicitly doubts some of her own claims and statements from her previous publication, further diminishing *On Photography*'s standing in photography theory.

Interaction

It has been 40 years since the publication of *On Photography*. During this time, there has been a tremendous change in how we observe photographic images with digital photography firmly supplanting the analogue photography of Sontag's time. Consequently, we as readers today no longer hold the same belief in the truth claims made about photography by a 1970s viewer or reader. Challenging these claims could be considered original in the 1970s at the time in which the book was written. Today, this form of critique is dated and there are few recent publications which have confronted or directly interacted with the outmoded arguments presented in *On Photography*. Nevertheless, the work is often perceived as inspirational. As film critic A.O. Scott* wrote in 2011, "It is almost literally an antediluvian book, dating from a time just before the digital revolution unleashed a flood of images upon the world beyond anything Sontag or her editors could have imagined."[3]

Sontag's assertion that as photographic images gained acceptance into the fine art museum context "they become studies in the possibilities of photography … and thus less about the subject of the images," was built upon further by Michael Fried.[4] Specifically referencing large-format contemporary art photographs, Fried elaborates on the relationship between the subject of the image, the viewer, and the dialogue each has with the art of the past, rather than on the political and social content of the image.[5]

Aside from her discussion of fine art photography, it could also be argued—though the author could not have predicted this—that *On Photography* pre-empted the work of sociologists who critique social media. Sontag's description of photography as something that offers, "in one easy, habit-forming activity, both participation and alienation in our own lives and those of others—allowing us to participate, while confirming alienation" prophetically foreshadows our interaction with photo-sharing social media platforms such as Facebook and Instagram.[6] Sociologist P. J. Rey* has considered the implications described by Sontag in more depth in a recent article "Alienation, Exploitation, and Social Media" published in 2012 in the peer reviewed journal, *American Behavioral Scientist*.[7]

The Continuing Debate

Under the guise of studies in documentary photography, contemporary academics continue to consider the problems of a photograph's claims to reality which was so central to Sontag's work.[8] However, much more prominent are questions pertaining to the mechanisms with which photographs elicit affect, and how they are circulated and consumed, primarily in a digital format. These preoccupations form the core of the contemporary intellectual debate surrounding the issues presented in *On Photography*.

In the book, Sontag expresses doubts about any tangible societal benefits or improvements to be had from photojournalism (and the work of photojournalists). When she writes that "to take a picture is to have an interest in things as they are, in the status quo remaining unchanged (at least for as long as it takes to get a 'good' picture) ... including, when that is the interest, another person's pain or misfortune," Sontag highlights a certain maliciousness in the work of press photographers.[9] In both histories of photography and in political science* today, academics analyze the effect of press images in relation to politically charged events, most often warfare. In doing so, they indirectly offer a response to Sontag's critique. In this context, political scientist David Campbell has defended the value of press photographs, stressing that they can become a repository of awareness which makes it all the more difficult for the viewer to continue on with a "moral defectiveness of ignorance or innocence in the face of suffering."[10]

NOTES

1   See Michael Starenko, "Sontag's Reception," *Afterimage* 25, no. 5 (1998): 6.

2   Sohnya Sayres, "In Summa: The Latter Essays – an Appreciation," in *The Scandal of Susan Sontag* (New York: Columbia University Press, 2009), 211.

3   A.O. Scott, "On (Digital) Photography: Sontag, 34 Years Later," *New York Times Magazine*, May 6, 2011, accessed February 1, 2013, http://www.nytimes.com/2011/05/08/magazine/mag-08Riff-t.html?pagewanted=all.

4   Susan Sontag, *On Photography*, 5th edn (New York: Farrar, Straus & Giroux, 2011), 133.

5   See Michael Fried, *Why Photography Matters as Art as Never Before* (New Haven, CT: Yale University Press, 2008).

6   Sontag, *On Photography*, 167.

7   P. J. Rey, "Alienation, exploitation, and social media," *American Behavioral Scientist* 56, no. 4 (2012): 399-420.

8   see Abigail Solomon-Godeau e.g. *Photography after Photography* (Durham and London: Duke University Press, 2017).

9   Sontag, *On Photography*, 12.

10 David Campbell, "Cultural Governance and Pictorial Resistance: Reflections on the Imaging of War," *Review of International Studies* 29, no. 1 (2003), accessed January 19, 2013, http://www.carnegiecouncil.org/publications/journal/17_2/review_essays/1029.html. When referring to "moral defectiveness" he is quoting Sontag: see Susan Sontag, *On Photography*, 5th edn (New York: Farrar, Straus & Giroux, 2011), 11. See also Susan Sontag, "War and Photography," in *Human Rights, Human Wrongs: The Oxford Amnesty Lectures* 2001, ed. N.J. Owen (Oxford: Oxford University Press, 2003), 272.

MODULE 12
WHERE NEXT?

KEY POINTS

- *On Photography* has the potential to be a viable tool in helping us understand the way we interact with photographic images today.
- Susie Linfield, Ariella Azoulay, and Geoff Dyer* have recently re-visited and re-invigorated Sontag's ideas.
- Its stylish writing and quotable aphorisms make the book a good read for anyone interested in the subject.

Potential

There's no doubt that *On Photography* is a pioneering book in the field of photographic criticism. It is also a multidisciplinary work that straddles the worlds of criticism, journalism, and academia, and which will likely remain a classic. While scholars involved in the academic realm of photography theory are now less likely to cite the work directly (although it is still alluded to), those outside the discipline have used Susan Sontag's text in productive ways which will likely continue.[1] The manner in which we have been transformed "into image junkies" and the argument that photography is "the most irresistible form of mental pollution" are still important considerations today, especially when discussing the ubiquity of digital media.[2]

Film critic and journalist A. O. Scott calls *On Photography* a jarringly prescient work because of the way it pre-empts the flood of computerized images and provides prophetic analysis regarding the characteristics of image-making in the digital age we now live in.[3] He states: "as we learn to negotiate the landscape of digital culture, [Sontag's] history of photography can provide a compass and a map."[4]

> **"** The conservationist remedy has not been applied, though. On the contrary, we have become, it seems, since the publication of *On Photography*, ever more profligate in the production and consumption of images, comprehensively excluding the real world from the one of images. **"**
>
> Marc Furstenau,* *Post Script - Essays in Film and the Humanities*

We make images faster today than ever before, through cameras— often those that come as part of our cell phones—but also through editing software like photoshop which allows us to manipulate images in a way that was unimaginable in the 1970s. As Sontag predicted, it is increasingly facile to render infinite constructions of the real. It has therefore become more relevant for us to question, in Sontag's words, the way in which we "shed light on [our] social order by atomizing it [into images]."[5] Photographs continue to be re-contextualized in the digital age, and it is still pressing to consider the way new contexts, such as the Internet, shape our perceptions of the images we are consuming.

Future Directions

In contemporary photographic theory today, Susie Linfield is perhaps the biggest exponent of the ideas presented in *On Photography*. Her book, *The Cruel Radiance*, frequently references On Photography and Sontag, and insists on the book's long-standing influence. Linfield credits *On Photography* as an incisive cornerstone of photographic criticism which has paved the way for a productive consideration of press photography, specifically images of catastrophe. Linfield demeans several of the photographic critics who followed in Sontag's footsteps. She describes Allan Sekula and Douglas Crimp as "postmodern and poststructuralist* children of Sontag [who] weren't really alive to photographs per se, much less to the world they reveal."[7] Instead, Linfield believes Sontag was an important theorist, influential in forming our understanding of how photography can be engaged with civically. In *Civil Imagination: A Political Ontology of Photography* (2012), Ariella Azoulay similarly re-engages with Sontag's discussion of the press photographer's interaction with his or her subject. Azoulay stresses that photographs taken in this capacity can reinforce, but also resist, the oppression confronting the sitters.[7] Both authors remain active in the field.

English writer Geoff Dyer's *The Ongoing Moment* (2005) re-invigorates Sontag's writing with a similar style and content to *On Photography*. He cites the challenge of actively trying to avoid quoting Sontag every five pages.[8] Like Sontag, he confesses to not being an expert in the field or owning a camera. In the same vein as *On Photography,* he created an eclectic and purposefully incomplete mediation on the medium.

Summary

Susan Sontag's *On Photography* is considered, with good reason, to be one of the most influential books published on the topic of photography. It is worth reading as a riveting polemic on the aesthetics and ethics of photography that highlights the deep impact photographs have on the way we live.

As one of Sontag's most important non-fiction books, delivered at the prime of her career, *On Photography* questions the so-called democratization of the medium, the way in which it portrays reality, and the truth of such a portrayal. It was the first work in the field to argue that snapping photos was a violation of the subject being photographed, and the first book to argue that capturing photos supported global capitalism (thus being a form of anti-interventionism). Sontag raised important queries about the role of photography in tourists' hands, in museums, and in the context of photojournalism.

She compared photography with painting in a dynamic and previously unconsidered fashion, questioned the way that photographs isolate and distance the viewer from the subject, and defined how the medium powerfully combines magic and information. Sontag's call for 'an ecology of images' has gone utterly unheeded, nevertheless, as the critic Jed Perl has recently argued, "Juggling the rival claims of photographs both as art objects and social documents, Sontag makes arguments that are even more striking today than they were a generation ago."[9]

On Photography has been reprinted and published in many languages. It remains one of the seminal texts published on the topic of photography. It is notable for both its pioneering analysis of the photograph's capabilities and the way in which it first sounded the alarm against the deluge of digital photographs which continue to define us as image-junkies who still live in Plato's Cave.

NOTES

1   For two noteworthy examples, see David Campbell, "Cultural Governance and Pictorial Resistance: Reflections on the Imaging of War," *Review of International Studies*, 29, no. 1 (2003): 57–73, and A.O. Scott, "On (Digital) Photography: Sontag, 34 Years Later," *New York Times Magazine*, May 6, 2011, accessed February 1, 2013, http://www.nytimes.com/2011/05/08/magazine/mag-08Riff-t.html?pagewanted=all.

2   Susan Sontag, *On Photography*, 5th edn (New York: Farrar, Straus & Giroux, 2011), 24.

3   A.O. Scott, "On (Digital) Photography"

4   Scott, "On (Digital) Photography".

5   Sontag, *On Photography*, 60.

6   Susie Linfield, *The Cruel Radiance: Photography and Political Violence* (Chicago: University of Chicago Press, 2011), 7-8

7   Ariella Azoulay. *Civil Imagination: a Political Ontology of Photography.* (London: Verso Books, 2015).

8   Geoff Dyer, *The Ongoing Moment* (Edinburgh: Canongate Books, 2005), 10.

9   Jed Perl, "The Middle Distance," *New Republic*, May 4, 2012, accessed
    December 12, 2012, http://www.newrepublic.com/article/books-and-arts/
    magazine/103068/susan-sontag-journals-notebooks-consciousness-
    harnessed-flesh.

GLOSSARY

GLOSSARY OF TERMS

2003 Invasion of Iraq: the American offensive that represented the start of the Iraq War. It was a major combat operation which deposed Saddam Hussein's government.

Abu Ghraib: a prison located close to Baghdad, Iraq where US military forces committed human rights abuses and systematic torture against detainees during the US occupation of Iraq between approximately 2003 and 2004. The photographs of said torture were widely circulated and caused an international uproar. Sontag wrote about them in her article, "Regarding the Torture of Others," which was published in the *New York Times Magazine* in 2004.

Affect theory: a psychological school of thought that attempts to organize emotions or feelings (affects) categorically in co-ordination with the responses these affects elicit.

American War in Vietnam (1959–75): a prolonged conflict between the United States of America and nationalist Vietnamese forces that were attempting to unite Vietnam under a communist regime.

Aura: a concept developed by Walter Benjamin that describes an object's uniqueness and authenticity, and withers if an object is mechanically reproduced.

BBC: the British Broadcasting Company, a British organization that makes television and radio programs.

Bergen–Belsen: a Nazi concentration camp during World War II, located in northern Germany.

Canon: the categorized set of literature, art, and music that is perceived as fundamental to Western culture.

Capitalism: an economic system that emphasizes the private ownership of the means of production. The means of production refers to those things, such as land, natural resources, and technology that are necessary to produce goods.

Colonialism: the practice of one country generating political control over another, primarily through settlers, occupation, and the subsequent maintenance of control over the occupied country.

Commodity fetishism: A principle espoused by Marx in chapter 1 of *Capital* which ultimately stresses the inevitability of measuring the value of things with money.

Concentration camps: internment prisons run by the Nazis during World War II that were primarily used to imprison and kill Jews, criminals, Romani, and homosexuals.

Cultural studies: an academic field that focuses in on the political dynamics of contemporary cultures with a specific emphasis on their historical foundations and defining traits. The field intersects sociology, cultural anthropology, ethnology, and the arts, among other disciplines.

Critical theory: a Marxist sociological and political line of enquiry espoused by the Frankfurt School. It stresses developing a critique of society and culture through the application of knowledge from the humanities and social sciences.

Dachau: the first concentration camp opened by the Nazis in Bavaria (southern Germany) to hold political prisoners. It was opened in 1933.

Death Mask: a conceptualization developed by Walter Benjamin that confers importance to the afterlife of a literary work (i.e. its existence after completion).

Ethical Citizenship: connotes having a sense of morality and acting in a civically engaged way.

Feminism: the belief in, and advocacy for, social, economic, and political equality of the sexes.

Feminist: being a feminist means advocating women's rights and the equality of the sexes, usually through the establishment of social, political, and economic rights for the female sex.

Formalism: in the context of art criticism, this describes assessing art based on what it is made of and what it looks like.

Frankfurt School: a school of critical philosophy affiliated with the Goethe University, Frankfurt. Notable affiliates include Theodor Adorno, Max Horkheimer, Herbert Marcuse, and Walter Benjamin. Sontag's writing in *On Photography* is inspired by the Frankfurt School's theories and she dedicates the entire last chapter of the book to Benjamin.

French Theory: A school of literary, social, and philosophical thought that appeared in French universities from the 1960s and the US from the 1970s where it had a strong influence in the artistic and activist communities. Major French progenitors include Jean Baudrillard, Simone de Beauvoir, Gilles Deleuze, Jacques Derrida, Michel Foucault, and Jacques Lacan. Frequently associated American authors of *French Theory* include Judith Butler, Gayatri Chakravorty Spivak, Fredric Jameson, and Donna Haraway.

Gonzo journalism: first used to describe an article in 1970 by Hunter S. Thompson and popularized by him thereafter, gonzo journalism is both a method of inquiry and a journalistic writing style which does not have a claim to objectivity. The journalist is usually the protagonist of his story and writing it in the first person.

Great Depression (1929-1939): The longest and most severe economic depression ever experienced by the industrialized Western world. Originating in the United States, the Great Depression caused severe unemployment and deflation throughout the world with staggering social and cultural effects. It also prompted fundamental changes to economic policy and theory.

Hermeneutics: the branch of knowledge that deals with interpretation, especially of the Bible or literary texts.

Indexical: a semiotic theory that originated from the writing of C. S. Pierce. Indexicality refers to having an index, also known as a *sign*, pointing to, or indexing, an object in the context where it occurs.

International Affairs: also known as foreign affairs or international relations, an interdisciplinary academic field that focuses on the relationships between political entities across international borders and the wider global systems produced by those interactions.

Marxism: a line of political, sociological, and economic thinking based on the ideas of Karl Marx, Friedrich Engels (to a lesser extent), and their followers. In the political context, Marxism is based on the notion of class struggle to attain a classless society, eventually arriving at an alternative to capitalism.

Marxist theory: the use of Marxist principles, primarily in Academic writing. This was applied by Walter Benjamin and in Susan Sontag's writing.

Modernism: a form of arts criticism popularized by Michael Fried and Clement Greenberg which claimed that art should engage in self-criticism to sustain itself, and for its own self-preservation. It thus becomes self-referential.

The Nation: the oldest weekly published magazine in the US. It covers liberal cultural analysis and news. Sontag was a contributor to *The Nation*.

Neo-Marxism: late twentieth century variances of Marxism that integrated contemporaneous intellectual approaches such as critical theory with Marxist theories.

The New Left: a political movement in the 1960s and 70s which opposed US military involvement in Vietnam and sought social change when it came to issues such as gay rights and abortion. Herbert Marcuse has been described as the progenitor of the movement.

New York Review of Books: a bi-weekly magazine founded in 1963 that features articles on literature, culture, and current affairs. It is based on the assumption that the discussion of books is a requisite literary activity and is one of the most well regarded magazines, globally, for the review of books. Sontag was a contributor.

The New Yorker: an important weekly US periodical founded in 1925 by Harold Ross and Jane Grant. While it focuses primarily on New York cultural events, the publication is internationally recognized for its reportage, political and social commentary, poetry, satire, and cartoons. It is edited by Condé Nast. Sontag contributed to the publication throughout her career.

Northern Vietnamese: The Northern Vietnamese fought with the Viet Cong against the Americans and Southern Vietnamese during the American War in Vietnam. They were proponents of communism and were anti-imperialist.

October **(Magazine):** a quarterly magazine specializing in contemporary art theory and criticism published by MIT Press. Some of its contributors are among the most renowned names in the fields of art and criticism. It was founded in 1976 by Rosalind Krauss and Annette Michelson. Some of Sontag's ideas were indirectly referred to in the magazine in the late 1970s, although Sontag herself was not a contributor.

Ontology: the science or study of being; that branch of metaphysics concerned with the nature or essence of being or existence (*OED*).

The Partisan Review: a quarterly magazine published in the US from 1934 to 2003. Sontag wrote for the magazine during the 1960s when it was an important outlet for political and cultural discussions and literary debates. It worked as a springboard for Sontag by popularizing her writing.

Photo history: or history of photography, is an academic discipline that charts the trajectory of photography from its invention as a medium to its existence today.

Photo theory: a school of thought that attempts to understand the meaning of photography. Rosalind Krauss, Allan Sekula, and Abigail Solomon-Godeau are all well regarded photo-theorists who were inspired by Sontag's writing. *On Photography* is an early example of photo theory.

Plato's Cave: also known as Allegory of the Cave, was a story by Plato, a Greek philosopher, which appears in book VII of his work, *The Republic*. Prisoners are in a cave with no knowledge of the outside world. As things pass by outside, the prisoners see the shadows of these things on the wall and believe they are perceiving the actual things, actual entities. When one prisoner is released to the outside world, he doesn't believe the things outside are real. Eventually, his eyes adjust and he believes in the reality of his surroundings. Sontag postulates that we are still living in Plato's Cave and it is the title of the first chapter in *On Photography*. She argues that we are stuck believing in images of truth (photography) and not in reality itself.

Political science: an academic discipline that focuses on how government and politics operate domestically and internationally.

Post-modernism: the state, condition, or period subsequent to that which is modern. Specifically, in architecture, the arts, literature, politics, and so on, any of the various styles, concepts, or points of view involving a conscious departure from modernism, especially when characterized by a rejection of ideology and theory in favor of a plurality of values and techniques (OED).

Post-structuralism: theories that extended and critiqued notions of structuralism. It primarily refers to critical theorists and French philosophers who were internationally recognized in the 1960s and 1970s. Jacques Derrida and Michel Foucault were two prominent post-structuralist thinkers who influenced Sontag and her writing in

On Photography.

Psychoanalysis: a form of theory that investigates the interactivity between the conscious and unconscious elements of the mind. It puts emphasis on repressed fears through the interpretation of dreams. Sigmund Freud, an Austrian neurologist, established the discipline in the early 1890s.

Semiotics: the science of communication studied through the interpretation of signs and symbols as they operate in various fields (OED).

Structuralism: in anthropology, a methodology that puts forward an understanding of human culture as seen through the structures found in language.

Surrealism: a 20th-century avant-garde movement in art and literature which sought to release the creative potential of the unconscious mind, for example by the irrational juxtaposition of images.

Susan Sontag Foundation: an entity that honors emerging artists in different disciplines and is devoted to promoting an exchange of language and culture internationally in the spirit of Susan Sontag. David Rieff is its president and the artist Marina Abramovic is on the board of directors.

UCLA: the University of California, Los Angeles, a public research university in LA, in the US, which is among the most important and prestigious universities in the world.

Uncanny: something that seems supernatural, strange, or mysterious.

Visual studies: an interdisciplinary research area born in the wake of cultural studies. It analyzes how vision is structured, notions of the gaze, and how images of contemporary cinema are manufactured, with an emphasis on American cinema.

World War II (1939-1945): an armed conflict between the Allied States (most significantly this included the UK and British Empire States, the US, France, and Russia) and the Powers of the Axis (mainly Nazi Germany, the Empire of Japan, and Italy). It was global in scale as war operations involved most nations on the planet. It is considered the most expansive armed conflict in history and totaled more than 60 million deaths. The Allied States were victorious.

Yugoslavian Civil War (1991–2001): also known as the Yugoslav Wars, a chain of interrelated military conflicts lasting 10 years that concluded in the dissolution of Yugoslavia and the establishment of autonomous states that were previously constituents of Yugoslavia. The conflict was mostly ethnically based and resulted in the deaths of approximately 140,000 people.

PEOPLE MENTIONED IN THE TEXT

Diane Arbus (1923–71) was an American portrait photographer known for her black-and-white images of misfits and abnormal people. Sontag speaks of her photographic work in a disparaging fashion for a substantial amount of *On Photography*.

Hannah Arendt (1906–75) was a German American intellectual and political theorist whose work primarily dealt with issues such as totalitarianism. She selected essays by Walter Benjamin for a significant anthology of the author's writing that Sontag would likely have read.

Ariella Azoulay (b. 1962) is an independent curator and photography theorist. She has written on the ethical and political aspects of photography.

Roland Barthes (1915–80) was a French semiotician, theorist, and critic who was known for his description of the importance of signs and symbols, especially in the realm of mass media. His book *Camera Lucida* is, along with *On Photography*, considered to be one of the more pioneering books of photo theory.

André Bazin (1918–58) was a French film theorist and critic. His influential ideas were published in the magazine he helped found, *Cahiers du Cinéma*.

Walter Benjamin (1892–1940) was a German philosopher, theorist, radio broadcaster, and translator. His politically oriented aesthetic theories are important components of art history and cultural studies.

John Berger (1926-2017) was an art critic, poet, and novelist. His book, *Ways of Seeing* was turned into a TV series and is used as a university textbook. His writing on photography remains influential.

David Campbell (b. 1971) is an author and political science professor. His specialties include political behavior and civic engagement.

Douglas Crimp (b. 1944) is an American art historian, critic, and former curator. He is the former co-editor of the renowned contemporary art journal *October*. He is known for his research on AIDS and its relation to culture.

Piotr A. Cieplak (b. 1960) is a renowned Polish cultural studies journalist and theatre director. He has written about images of death and genocide.

Luc Delahaye (b. 1962) is a photographer. His images are often melancholic and his photography straddles the boundary between press imagery and art. His photographs have received recognition in the form of major museum and commercial gallery exhibitions.

Guy Debord (1931-94) was a French philosopher known for his Marxist theories. His most well-known book was *The Society of the Spectacle* which charts how modern society has been developed through notions of representation.

Jacques Derrida (1930-2004) was a philosopher of French origin known for the development of deconstruction, his trademark form of semiotic analysis. His writing had an influence on Sontag's.

Geoff Dyer (b. 1958) is an English author who has written various non-fiction works and novels. His book, *The Ongoing Moment,* bears certain affinities with *On Photography* in the sense that it is a broad overview of the photographic medium written by someone who is not an expert in the field.

Jae Emerling (b. 1945) is an author known for his writing in the realm of art history. He has written in depth about the history of photography and photo theory.

Walker Evans (1903-75) was an American photographer known for his documentarian images. His most recognizable series is his photojournalistic work covering the Great Depression.

Michael Fried (b. 1939) is an art critic and poet known for his art history writing, which contributed to debates surrounding modernism in Western visual art. His formalist approach to examining photography was a predecessor to Sontag's postmodern inclinations when it came to writing about the medium.

Michel Foucault (1926-84) was a French philosopher and social critic. He had a significant impact on both structuralist and post-structuralist ways of thinking. His writing on the panopticon mirrored Sontag's approach to analyzing photography.

Marc Furstenau is a professor of Film Studies at Carlton University. He has published on cinema and semiotics, film theory, on the philosophical cinema of Terrence Malick, and on the photographic theory of Susan Sontag. He is co-editor of the Canadian Journal of Film Studies.

Clement Greenberg (1909-94) was an American art critic of immense influence and one of the most well-known critics of the twentieth century. His prose focused on the formal appearance of an artwork. This contrasted Sontag's criticism which was postmodernist, and detailed the circumstances behind the production of an artwork and its societal implications.

Rosalind Krauss (b. 1941) is an American art critic and art theorist known for helping to establish *October* and for her mode of criticism, which integrates Freudian psychoanalysis and the theories of Clement Greenberg.

Claude Lévi-Strauss (1908-2009) used structural analysis to develop his original variation of social anthropology. His work influenced writing on film and photography.

David Levi Strauss (b. 1953) is a poet and cultural critic who has written various artist monographs as well as numerous essays on photography. He has claimed that, for him, *On Photography* opened new possibilities for photographic criticism.

Michael Lesy (b. 1945) is a writer and professor of journalism. He penned one of the most antagonising responses to *On Photography* which was predicated on his perception that Sontag had never actually used a camera before.

Susie Linfield (b. 1955) is a professor of journalism and cultural critic. She has written about photography with a specific focus on images of torture and war in a way that continues the trajectory of criticism that Sontag had initiated with *On Photography*.

Simon Malpas (b. 1968) is a professor of English literature. His expertise includes postmodernism and contemporary theatre. He has written about how Sontag's assessment of the societal function of photography is comparable to Foucault's description of the panopticon.

Mary McCarthy (1912–89) was an American political activist and author. She contributed to many of the same publications that Sontag did and, like Sontag, was viewed as a New York intellectual with strong leftist proclivities.

John McCole is a professor of history who is known for his writing on Walter Benjamin and Max Horkheimer. He has written multiple articles that responded to *On Photography*.

Jed Perl (b. 1951) is a renowned American art critic. He reviewed the first published anthology of Sontag's journal entries and has referred to her in numerous reviews.

Plato (c.427 B.C.E.–c.347 B.C.E.) was a Greek philosopher. He is one of the most widely recognized names in philosophy and his influence in Western philosophical thought is unparalleled. He explored notions of beauty, aesthetics, justice, theology, and cosmology. His Allegory of the Cave is referenced by Sontag and used by her as a metaphor to describe the way in which we perceive photographs as being true representations of reality.

P. J. Rey (b. 1984) is a sociology doctoral candidate. His writing considers the ways in which new forms of communication, including the use of social media, have altered the cultural and economic landscape of the US.

David Rieff (b. 1952) is an author of non-fiction and Susan Sontag's son. Like his mother, he has devoted a large amount of his writing to issues of humanitarianism and international conflict. He has published Sontag's journals posthumously and is the president of the Susan Sontag Foundation.

Philip Rieff (1922–2006) was an American cultural critic and influential sociologist. He was Susan Sontag's professor, and her first and only husband.

Martha Rosler (b. 1943) is an American artist and writer. Her work is primarily photographic and/or film based. She has been a leading critical feminist voice throughout her career.

Charles Ruas (b. 1938) is an American art critic and author. He is well known for his work as an interviewer. He interviewed Sontag for the *New York Times* in 1982.

Sebastião Salgado (b. 1944) is a Brazilian photographer. His work is photojournalistic and he tends to seek out unsettling scenes and subjects which are mostly shot in black and white.

A. O. Scott (b. 1966) is the chief film critic for the *New York Times*. He has written about the way in which digital photography today has fulfilled some of the predictions Sontag made in *On Photography*.

Sohnya Sayers is an American humanities professor who lectures and writes on cultural issues. She wrote *Susan Sontag: The Elegiac Modernist*, a full-length study on Sontag's life and work that was first published in 1990.

Allan Sekula (1951-2013) was an American photographer and filmmaker. He was also a photo-critic and photo-theorist. Through his photography and writing he explored the implications of capitalism, global trade, and macroeconomics.

Michael Starenko is a learning instructor, media studies expert, and former editor-in-chief of *Afterimage*, a well-regarded photography and media studies journal. He wrote an article that discussed the reception of Sontag's *On Photography* twenty years after it was initially published.

Abigail Solomon-Godeau (b. 1948) is an American art historian who specializes in feminist theory and contemporary art. She is well known for her photographic criticism which drew inspiration from Sontag's writing.

Edward Steichen (1879-1973) was a highly influential American photographer and curator. He was one of the most important figures of twentieth century American photography. As a curator, he helped facilitate the entrance of photography into fine art museums.

John Szarkowski (1925–2007) was a well-known curator and critic. He was the head curator of the Museum of Modern Art in New York City from 1962 to 1991.

Paul Wake (b. 1973) is an author and professor who specializes in narrative theory and both analogue and digital games. He is a co-editor of the Routledge Companion to Critical and Cultural Theory.

Walt Whitman (1819-92) was an important American poet and essayist. His notions of humanism were significant to Sontag and he is referred to throughout the second chapter of *On Photography*.

A. C. Vroman (1856-1916) was an American photographer and visual artist. He was known for his ethnographic work on Native Americans.

WORKS CITED

WORKS CITED

Azoulay, Ariella. *The Civil Contract of Photography*. Cambridge, MA: MIT Press, 2012.

— *Civil Imagination: a Political Ontology of Photography*. London: Verso Books, 2015.

Barthes, Roland. *Camera Lucida: Reflections on Photography*. New York: Farrar, Straus & Giroux, 1981.

— *Mythologies*. Translated by Annette Lavers. New York: Farrar, Straus & Giroux, 1972.

Basu, Manisha. "The Hamartia of Light and Shadow: Susan Sontag in the Digital Age." *Postmodern Culture* 16, no. 3 (2006): n.p.

Bazin, André. "The Ontology of the Photographic Image." In *What is Cinema?, Volume 1*. Translated by Hugo Gray, 9-16. Oakland: University of California Press, 2005.

Benjamin, Walter. *The Arcades Project*. Translated by Howard Eiland and Kevin McLaughlin and prepared on the basis of the German Volume edited by Rolf Tiedemann. Cambridge, MA: Harvard University Press, 1999.

"A Short History of Photography." *Screen,* Volume 13, Issue 1 (March 1, 1972): 5-26.

Benjamin, Walter, and Hannah Arendt. *Illuminations*. Translated by Harry Zohn. New York: Knopf Doubleday, 1969.

Bennett, Jill. *Empathic Vision: Affect, Trauma, and Contemporary Art*. Stanford: Stanford University Press, 2005.

Berger, John. *About Looking*. London: Bloomsbury, 2009.

— "Uses of Photography: For Susan Sontag" In *Understanding a Photograph,* edited by Geoff Dyer, 49-60. London: Penguin, 2013.

Campbell, David. "Cultural Governance and Pictorial Resistance: Reflections on the Imaging of War." *Review of International Studies* 29, no. 1 (2003): 57–73. Accessed February 5, 2013. https://www.david-campbell.org/wp-content/documents/Cultural_Governance.pdf.

— "Representing Contemporary War." *Ethics and International Affairs* 17, no. 2 (2003): 99–108.

Cieplak, Piotr A. "The Canon. *On Photography* by Susan Sontag." *Times Higher Education* (October 22, 2009). Accessed January 10, 2013. http://www.timeshighereducation.co.uk/408739.article.

Crimp, Douglas. *Pictures*. New York: Artists Space; Committee for the Visual Arts, 1977.

Debord, Guy. *The Society of the Spectacle*. New York: Zone Books, 1994.

Delahaye, Luc. *Winterreise*. London: Phaidon, 2003.

Drenttel, William. "In Remembrance of Susan Sontag." *Observatory*, December 29, 2004. Accessed February 7, 2013. http://designobserver.com/feature/in-remembrance-of-susan-sontag/2877.

Dyer, Geoff. *The Ongoing Moment*. Edinburgh: Canongate Books, 2005.

Edwards, Susan E. "Photography and the Representation of the Other: A Discussion Inspired by the Work of Sebastião Salgado." *Third Text* 5, no. 16–17 (1991): 157–72.

Eisinger, Joel. *Trace and Transformation: American Criticism of Photography in the Modernist Period*. Albuquerque: University of New Mexico Press, 1999.

Fontcuberta, Joan, and Hubertus von Amelunxen. *Photography: Crisis of History*. Barcelona: Actar, 2004.

Fox, Margalit. "Susan Sontag, Social Critic With Verve, Dies at 71." *New York Times*, December 28, 2004. Accessed September 28, 2017. http://www.nytimes.com/2004/12/28/books/susan-sontag-social-critic-with-verve-dies-at-71.html?mcubz=1.

Fried, Michael. "Art and Objecthood." *Artforum* (June 1967). Reprinted in Gregory Battcock, ed., *Minimal Art: A Critical Anthology*. New York: Dutton (1968): 116–47.

— *Why Photography Matters as Art as Never Before*. New Haven, CT: Yale University Press, 2008.

Garlick, Steve. "Revealing the Unseen: Tourism, Art and Photography." *Cultural Studies* 16, no. 2 (2002): 289–305.

Goldberg, Vicki. *Photography in Print: Writings from 1816 to the Present*. Albuquerque: University of New Mexico Press Press, 1981.

Greenhouse, Emily. "Can We Ever Know Sontag?" *New Yorker Blog*, April 25, 2012. Accessed December 19, 2012. http://www.newyorker.com/online/blogs/books/2012/04/can-we-ever-know-sontag.html.

Grossman, Edward. "False Images." *Saturday Review* (December 10, 1977): 46–8. Accessed December 13, 2012. http://www.unz.org/Pub/SaturdayRev-1977dec10-00046?View=PDFPages.

Krauss, Rosalind. "Photography's Discursive Spaces: Landscape/View." *Art Journal* 42, no. 4 (Winter 1982): 311–19.

Krauss, Rosalind, and Annette Michelson. "Photography: A Special Issue." *October* 5 (Summer 1978): 3–7.

Lesy, Michael. "An Unacknowledged Autobiography." *Afterimage* 5, no. 7 (January 1978): 5.

Linfield, Susie. *The Cruel Radiance: Photography and Political Violence*. Chicago: University of Chicago Press, 2011.

Malpas, Simon and Paul Wake, eds., *The Routledge Companion to Critical and Cultural Theory*. New York: Routledge, 2013.

McCole, John. "Walter Benjamin, Susan Sontag, and the Radical Critique of Photography." *Afterimage* 7.1–2 (Summer 1979): 12-14.

McRobbie, Angela. *Postmodernism and Popular Culture*. London and New York: Routledge, 1994.

Mitrano, G.F. "The Photographic Imagination: Sontag and Benjamin." *Post Script* 26, no. 2 (2007): 117.

Movius, Geoffrey. "An Interview with Susan Sontag." *Boston Review*, (June 1975). Accessed January 19, 2013. http://bostonreview.net/susan-sontag-interview-geoffrey-movius.

Peirce, C.S. *Collected Papers of Charles Sanders Peirce*. Cambridge, MA: Belknap Press of Harvard University Press, 1958.

Perl, Jed. "The Middle Distance." *New Republic*, May 4, 2012. Accessed December 12, 2013. http://www.newrepublic.com/article/books-and-arts/magazine/103068/susan-sontag-journals-notebooks-consciousness-harnessed-flesh.

Plato. *The Republic*. Penguin Classics. Harmondsworth: Penguin, 2007.

Rey, P.J. "Alienation, exploitation, and social media." *American Behavioral Scientist* 56, no. 4 (2012): 399-420.

Rieff, David. *Swimming in a Sea of Death: A Son's Memoir*. New York: Simon & Schuster, 2008.

Rollyson, Carl, and Lisa Paddock. "My Desert Childhood." In *Susan Sontag: The Making of an Icon*. New York: W.W. Norton, 2000.

Rosler, Martha. "In, Around, and Afterthoughts (on Documentary Photography)." In *Decoys and Distruptions: Selected Writings, 1975–2001*: 151–207. Cambridge, MA: MIT Press, 2004.

— "Lookers, Buyers, Dealers and Makers: Thoughts on Audience." In *Decoys and Disruptions: Selected Writings, 1975–2001*: 9–53. Cambridge, MA: MIT Press, 2004.

Ruas, Charles. "Susan Sontag: Pas, Present and Future." *The New York Times*, October 24, 1982. Accessed August 15, 2017. http://www.nytimes.com/books/00/03/12/specials/sontag-past.html?mcubz=1.

Sayres, Sohnya. "In Summa: The Latter Essays—an Appreciation." In *The Scandal of Susan Sontag*: 215–36. New York: Columbia University Press, 2009.

Scott, A.O. "On (Digital) Photography: Sontag, 34 Years Later." *New York Times Magazine* (May 6, 2011). Accessed February 1, 2013. http://www.nytimes.com/2011/05/08/magazine/mag-08Riff-t.html?pagewanted=all.

Sekula, Allan. "On the Invention of Photographic Meaning." Ph.D. diss., University of California, San Diego, 1974.

— "The Traffic in Photographs." *Art Journal* 41, no. 1 (1981): 15–25. Sekula, Allan, and Ohio State University, Gallery of Fine Art.

Photography against the Grain: Essays and Photo Works, 1973–1983. Halifax: Press of Nova Scotia College of Art and Design, 1984.

Sentilles, Sarah. "Just Looking: Theological Language, Ethics, and Photographs of Violence." Ph.D. diss., Harvard University, 2008.

Siegel, Katy. "On Susan Sontag (1933–2004)." Obituary. *The Brooklyn Rail*. Accessed December 15, 2012. http://www.brooklynrail.org/2005/02/art/on-susan-sontag-1933-2004.

Solomon-Godeau, Abigail. *Photography at the Dock: Essays on Photographic History, Institutions, and Practices*. Minneapolis: University of Minnesota Press, 1991.

— *Photography after Photography*. Durham and London: Duke University Press, 2017.

Sontag, Susan. *Against Interpretation and Other Essays*. New York: Macmillan, 1966.

— "Looking at War: Photography's View of Devastation and Death". December 9, 2002. Accessed August 10, 2017. http://www.newyorker.com/magazine/2002/12/09/looking-at-war.

— *On Photography*. 5th edn. New York: Farrar, Straus & Giroux, 2011.

— *Regarding the Pain of Others*. New York: Picador, 2004.

— "Regarding the Torture of Others." *The New York Times Magazine*, May 23, 2004. Accessed August 19, 2017. http://www.nytimes.com/2004/05/23/magazine/regarding-the-torture-of-others.html?_r=0.

— *Styles of Radical Will*. London: Penguin, 2013.

— *rip to Hanoi*. New York: Farrar, Straus & Giroux, 1969.

— "Waiting for Godot in Sarajevo." *Performing Arts Journal* 16, no. 2 (1994): 87–106.

— "War and Photography." In *Human Rights, Human Wrongs: The Oxford Amnesty Lectures 2001*, ed. N.J. Owen, 253–78. Oxford: Oxford University Press, 2003.

Sontag, Susan, and David Rieff. *As Consciousness is Harnessed to Flesh: Journals and Notebooks, 1964–1980*. New York: Farrar, Straus & Giroux, 2012.

— *Reborn: Journals and Notebooks, 1947–1963*. New York: Farrar, Straus & Giroux, 2009.

Starenko, Michael. "Sontag's Reception." *Afterimage* 25, no. 5 (1998): 6.

The ASX Team, "Susan Sontag: Speech and Interview at Wellesley College" *American Suburb X*. June 11, 2013. Accessed August 18, 2017. http://www.americansuburbx.com/2013/06/susan-sontag-speech-and-inteview-at-wellesley-college-1975.html.

The Associated Press, "Sontag Sells her Papers to U.C.L.A." *The New York Times*, January 17, 2002. Accessed August 20, 2017 http://www.nytimes.com/2002/01/27/us/sontag-sells-her-papers-to-ucla.html?mcubz=1.

Wells, Liz. *Photography: A Critical Introduction*. London and New York: Routledge, 2004.

Williams, John. "Benjamin Moser to Write Sontag Biography." *New York Times*, February 27, 2013. Accessed March 1, 2013. http://artsbeat.blogs.nytimes.com/2013/02/27/benjamin-moser-to-write-sontag-biography/.

THE MACAT LIBRARY
BY DISCIPLINE

AFRICANA STUDIES

Chinua Achebe's *An Image of Africa: Racism in Conrad's Heart of Darkness*
W. E. B. Du Bois's *The Souls of Black Folk*
Zora Neale Huston's *Characteristics of Negro Expression*
Martin Luther King Jr's *Why We Can't Wait*
Toni Morrison's *Playing in the Dark: Whiteness in the American Literary Imagination*

ANTHROPOLOGY

Arjun Appadurai's *Modernity at Large: Cultural Dimensions of Globalisation*
Philippe Ariès's *Centuries of Childhood*
Franz Boas's *Race, Language and Culture*
Kim Chan & Renée Mauborgne's *Blue Ocean Strategy*
Jared Diamond's *Guns, Germs & Steel: the Fate of Human Societies*
Jared Diamond's *Collapse: How Societies Choose to Fail or Survive*
E. E. Evans-Pritchard's *Witchcraft, Oracles and Magic Among the Azande*
James Ferguson's *The Anti-Politics Machine*
Clifford Geertz's *The Interpretation of Cultures*
David Graeber's *Debt: the First 5000 Years*
Karen Ho's *Liquidated: An Ethnography of Wall Street*
Geert Hofstede's *Culture's Consequences: Comparing Values, Behaviors, Institutes and Organizations across Nations*
Claude Lévi-Strauss's *Structural Anthropology*
Jay Macleod's *Ain't No Makin' It: Aspirations and Attainment in a Low-Income Neighborhood*
Saba Mahmood's *The Politics of Piety: The Islamic Revival and the Feminist Subject*
Marcel Mauss's *The Gift*

BUSINESS

Jean Lave & Etienne Wenger's *Situated Learning*
Theodore Levitt's *Marketing Myopia*
Burton G. Malkiel's *A Random Walk Down Wall Street*
Douglas McGregor's *The Human Side of Enterprise*
Michael Porter's *Competitive Strategy: Creating and Sustaining Superior Performance*
John Kotter's *Leading Change*
C. K. Prahalad & Gary Hamel's *The Core Competence of the Corporation*

CRIMINOLOGY

Michelle Alexander's *The New Jim Crow: Mass Incarceration in the Age of Colorblindness*
Michael R. Gottfredson & Travis Hirschi's *A General Theory of Crime*
Richard Herrnstein & Charles A. Murray's *The Bell Curve: Intelligence and Class Structure in American Life*
Elizabeth Loftus's *Eyewitness Testimony*
Jay Macleod's *Ain't No Makin' It: Aspirations and Attainment in a Low-Income Neighborhood*
Philip Zimbardo's *The Lucifer Effect*

ECONOMICS

Janet Abu-Lughod's *Before European Hegemony*
Ha-Joon Chang's *Kicking Away the Ladder*
David Brion Davis's *The Problem of Slavery in the Age of Revolution*
Milton Friedman's *The Role of Monetary Policy*
Milton Friedman's *Capitalism and Freedom*
David Graeber's *Debt: the First 5000 Years*
Friedrich Hayek's *The Road to Serfdom*
Karen Ho's *Liquidated: An Ethnography of Wall Street*

John Maynard Keynes's *The General Theory of Employment, Interest and Money*
Charles P. Kindleberger's *Manias, Panics and Crashes*
Robert Lucas's *Why Doesn't Capital Flow from Rich to Poor Countries?*
Burton G. Malkiel's *A Random Walk Down Wall Street*
Thomas Robert Malthus's *An Essay on the Principle of Population*
Karl Marx's *Capital*
Thomas Piketty's *Capital in the Twenty-First Century*
Amartya Sen's *Development as Freedom*
Adam Smith's *The Wealth of Nations*
Nassim Nicholas Taleb's *The Black Swan: The Impact of the Highly Improbable*
Amos Tversky's & Daniel Kahneman's *Judgment under Uncertainty: Heuristics and Biases*
Mahbub Ul Haq's *Reflections on Human Development*
Max Weber's *The Protestant Ethic and the Spirit of Capitalism*

FEMINISM AND GENDER STUDIES

Judith Butler's *Gender Trouble*
Simone De Beauvoir's *The Second Sex*
Michel Foucault's *History of Sexuality*
Betty Friedan's *The Feminine Mystique*
Saba Mahmood's *The Politics of Piety: The Islamic Revival and the Feminist Subject*
Joan Wallach Scott's *Gender and the Politics of History*
Mary Wollstonecraft's *A Vindication of the Rights of Women*
Virginia Woolf's *A Room of One's Own*

GEOGRAPHY

The Brundtland Report's *Our Common Future*
Rachel Carson's *Silent Spring*
Charles Darwin's *On the Origin of Species*
James Ferguson's *The Anti-Politics Machine*
Jane Jacobs's *The Death and Life of Great American Cities*
James Lovelock's *Gaia: A New Look at Life on Earth*
Amartya Sen's *Development as Freedom*
Mathis Wackernagel & William Rees's *Our Ecological Footprint*

HISTORY

Janet Abu-Lughod's *Before European Hegemony*
Benedict Anderson's *Imagined Communities*
Bernard Bailyn's *The Ideological Origins of the American Revolution*
Hanna Batatu's *The Old Social Classes And The Revolutionary Movements Of Iraq*
Christopher Browning's *Ordinary Men: Reserve Police Batallion 101 and the Final Solution in Poland*
Edmund Burke's *Reflections on the Revolution in France*
William Cronon's *Nature's Metropolis: Chicago And The Great West*
Alfred W. Crosby's *The Columbian Exchange*
Hamid Dabashi's *Iran: A People Interrupted*
David Brion Davis's *The Problem of Slavery in the Age of Revolution*
Nathalie Zemon Davis's *The Return of Martin Guerre*
Jared Diamond's *Guns, Germs & Steel: the Fate of Human Societies*
Frank Dikotter's *Mao's Great Famine*
John W Dower's *War Without Mercy: Race And Power In The Pacific War*
W. E. B. Du Bois's *The Souls of Black Folk*
Richard J. Evans's *In Defence of History*
Lucien Febvre's *The Problem of Unbelief in the 16th Century*
Sheila Fitzpatrick's *Everyday Stalinism*

The Macat Library By Discipline

Eric Foner's *Reconstruction: America's Unfinished Revolution, 1863-1877*
Michel Foucault's *Discipline and Punish*
Michel Foucault's *History of Sexuality*
Francis Fukuyama's *The End of History and the Last Man*
John Lewis Gaddis's *We Now Know: Rethinking Cold War History*
Ernest Gellner's *Nations and Nationalism*
Eugene Genovese's *Roll, Jordan, Roll: The World the Slaves Made*
Carlo Ginzburg's *The Night Battles*
Daniel Goldhagen's *Hitler's Willing Executioners*
Jack Goldstone's *Revolution and Rebellion in the Early Modern World*
Antonio Gramsci's *The Prison Notebooks*
Alexander Hamilton, John Jay & James Madison's *The Federalist Papers*
Christopher Hill's *The World Turned Upside Down*
Carole Hillenbrand's *The Crusades: Islamic Perspectives*
Thomas Hobbes's *Leviathan*
Eric Hobsbawm's *The Age Of Revolution*
John A. Hobson's *Imperialism: A Study*
Albert Hourani's *History of the Arab Peoples*
Samuel P. Huntington's *The Clash of Civilizations and the Remaking of World Order*
C. L. R. James's *The Black Jacobins*
Tony Judt's *Postwar: A History of Europe Since 1945*
Ernst Kantorowicz's *The King's Two Bodies: A Study in Medieval Political Theology*
Paul Kennedy's *The Rise and Fall of the Great Powers*
Ian Kershaw's *The "Hitler Myth": Image and Reality in the Third Reich*
John Maynard Keynes's *The General Theory of Employment, Interest and Money*
Charles P. Kindleberger's *Manias, Panics and Crashes*
Martin Luther King Jr's *Why We Can't Wait*
Henry Kissinger's *World Order: Reflections on the Character of Nations and the Course of History*
Thomas Kuhn's *The Structure of Scientific Revolutions*
Georges Lefebvre's *The Coming of the French Revolution*
John Locke's *Two Treatises of Government*
Niccolò Machiavelli's *The Prince*
Thomas Robert Malthus's *An Essay on the Principle of Population*
Mahmood Mamdani's *Citizen and Subject: Contemporary Africa And The Legacy Of Late Colonialism*
Karl Marx's *Capital*
Stanley Milgram's *Obedience to Authority*
John Stuart Mill's *On Liberty*
Thomas Paine's *Common Sense*
Thomas Paine's *Rights of Man*
Geoffrey Parker's *Global Crisis: War, Climate Change and Catastrophe in the Seventeenth Century*
Jonathan Riley-Smith's *The First Crusade and the Idea of Crusading*
Jean-Jacques Rousseau's *The Social Contract*
Joan Wallach Scott's *Gender and the Politics of History*
Theda Skocpol's *States and Social Revolutions*
Adam Smith's *The Wealth of Nations*
Timothy Snyder's *Bloodlands: Europe Between Hitler and Stalin*
Sun Tzu's *The Art of War*
Keith Thomas's *Religion and the Decline of Magic*
Thucydides's *The History of the Peloponnesian War*
Frederick Jackson Turner's *The Significance of the Frontier in American History*
Odd Arne Westad's *The Global Cold War: Third World Interventions And The Making Of Our Times*

LITERATURE

Chinua Achebe's *An Image of Africa: Racism in Conrad's Heart of Darkness*
Roland Barthes's *Mythologies*
Homi K. Bhabha's *The Location of Culture*
Judith Butler's *Gender Trouble*
Simone De Beauvoir's *The Second Sex*
Ferdinand De Saussure's *Course in General Linguistics*
T. S. Eliot's *The Sacred Wood: Essays on Poetry and Criticism*
Zora Neale Huston's *Characteristics of Negro Expression*
Toni Morrison's *Playing in the Dark: Whiteness in the American Literary Imagination*
Edward Said's *Orientalism*
Gayatri Chakravorty Spivak's *Can the Subaltern Speak?*
Mary Wollstonecraft's *A Vindication of the Rights of Women*
Virginia Woolf's *A Room of One's Own*

PHILOSOPHY

Elizabeth Anscombe's *Modern Moral Philosophy*
Hannah Arendt's *The Human Condition*
Aristotle's *Metaphysics*
Aristotle's *Nicomachean Ethics*
Edmund Gettier's *Is Justified True Belief Knowledge?*
Georg Wilhelm Friedrich Hegel's *Phenomenology of Spirit*
David Hume's *Dialogues Concerning Natural Religion*
David Hume's *The Enquiry for Human Understanding*
Immanuel Kant's *Religion within the Boundaries of Mere Reason*
Immanuel Kant's *Critique of Pure Reason*
Søren Kierkegaard's *The Sickness Unto Death*
Søren Kierkegaard's *Fear and Trembling*
C. S. Lewis's *The Abolition of Man*
Alasdair MacIntyre's *After Virtue*
Marcus Aurelius's *Meditations*
Friedrich Nietzsche's *On the Genealogy of Morality*
Friedrich Nietzsche's *Beyond Good and Evil*
Plato's *Republic*
Plato's *Symposium*
Jean-Jacques Rousseau's *The Social Contract*
Gilbert Ryle's *The Concept of Mind*
Baruch Spinoza's *Ethics*
Sun Tzu's *The Art of War*
Ludwig Wittgenstein's *Philosophical Investigations*

POLITICS

Benedict Anderson's *Imagined Communities*
Aristotle's *Politics*
Bernard Bailyn's *The Ideological Origins of the American Revolution*
Edmund Burke's *Reflections on the Revolution in France*
John C. Calhoun's *A Disquisition on Government*
Ha-Joon Chang's *Kicking Away the Ladder*
Hamid Dabashi's *Iran: A People Interrupted*
Hamid Dabashi's *Theology of Discontent: The Ideological Foundation of the Islamic Revolution in Iran*
Robert Dahl's *Democracy and its Critics*
Robert Dahl's *Who Governs?*
David Brion Davis's *The Problem of Slavery in the Age of Revolution*

Alexis De Tocqueville's *Democracy in America*
James Ferguson's *The Anti-Politics Machine*
Frank Dikotter's *Mao's Great Famine*
Sheila Fitzpatrick's *Everyday Stalinism*
Eric Foner's *Reconstruction: America's Unfinished Revolution, 1863-1877*
Milton Friedman's *Capitalism and Freedom*
Francis Fukuyama's *The End of History and the Last Man*
John Lewis Gaddis's *We Now Know: Rethinking Cold War History*
Ernest Gellner's *Nations and Nationalism*
David Graeber's *Debt: the First 5000 Years*
Antonio Gramsci's *The Prison Notebooks*
Alexander Hamilton, John Jay & James Madison's *The Federalist Papers*
Friedrich Hayek's *The Road to Serfdom*
Christopher Hill's *The World Turned Upside Down*
Thomas Hobbes's *Leviathan*
John A. Hobson's *Imperialism: A Study*
Samuel P. Huntington's *The Clash of Civilizations and the Remaking of World Order*
Tony Judt's *Postwar: A History of Europe Since 1945*
David C. Kang's *China Rising: Peace, Power and Order in East Asia*
Paul Kennedy's *The Rise and Fall of Great Powers*
Robert Keohane's *After Hegemony*
Martin Luther King Jr.'s *Why We Can't Wait*
Henry Kissinger's *World Order: Reflections on the Character of Nations and the Course of History*
John Locke's *Two Treatises of Government*
Niccolò Machiavelli's *The Prince*
Thomas Robert Malthus's *An Essay on the Principle of Population*
Mahmood Mamdani's *Citizen and Subject: Contemporary Africa And The Legacy Of Late Colonialism*
Karl Marx's *Capital*
John Stuart Mill's *On Liberty*
John Stuart Mill's *Utilitarianism*
Hans Morgenthau's *Politics Among Nations*
Thomas Paine's *Common Sense*
Thomas Paine's *Rights of Man*
Thomas Piketty's *Capital in the Twenty-First Century*
Robert D. Putman's *Bowling Alone*
John Rawls's *Theory of Justice*
Jean-Jacques Rousseau's *The Social Contract*
Theda Skocpol's *States and Social Revolutions*
Adam Smith's *The Wealth of Nations*
Sun Tzu's *The Art of War*
Henry David Thoreau's *Civil Disobedience*
Thucydides's *The History of the Peloponnesian War*
Kenneth Waltz's *Theory of International Politics*
Max Weber's *Politics as a Vocation*
Odd Arne Westad's *The Global Cold War: Third World Interventions And The Making Of Our Times*

POSTCOLONIAL STUDIES

Roland Barthes's *Mythologies*
Frantz Fanon's *Black Skin, White Masks*
Homi K. Bhabha's *The Location of Culture*
Gustavo Gutiérrez's *A Theology of Liberation*
Edward Said's *Orientalism*
Gayatri Chakravorty Spivak's *Can the Subaltern Speak?*

PSYCHOLOGY

Gordon Allport's *The Nature of Prejudice*
Alan Baddeley & Graham Hitch's *Aggression: A Social Learning Analysis*
Albert Bandura's *Aggression: A Social Learning Analysis*
Leon Festinger's *A Theory of Cognitive Dissonance*
Sigmund Freud's *The Interpretation of Dreams*
Betty Friedan's *The Feminine Mystique*
Michael R. Gottfredson & Travis Hirschi's *A General Theory of Crime*
Eric Hoffer's *The True Believer: Thoughts on the Nature of Mass Movements*
William James's *Principles of Psychology*
Elizabeth Loftus's *Eyewitness Testimony*
A. H. Maslow's *A Theory of Human Motivation*
Stanley Milgram's *Obedience to Authority*
Steven Pinker's *The Better Angels of Our Nature*
Oliver Sacks's *The Man Who Mistook His Wife For a Hat*
Richard Thaler & Cass Sunstein's *Nudge: Improving Decisions About Health, Wealth and Happiness*
Amos Tversky's *Judgment under Uncertainty: Heuristics and Biases*
Philip Zimbardo's *The Lucifer Effect*

SCIENCE

Rachel Carson's *Silent Spring*
William Cronon's *Nature's Metropolis: Chicago And The Great West*
Alfred W. Crosby's *The Columbian Exchange*
Charles Darwin's *On the Origin of Species*
Richard Dawkin's *The Selfish Gene*
Thomas Kuhn's *The Structure of Scientific Revolutions*
Geoffrey Parker's *Global Crisis: War, Climate Change and Catastrophe in the Seventeenth Century*
Mathis Wackernagel & William Rees's *Our Ecological Footprint*

SOCIOLOGY

Michelle Alexander's *The New Jim Crow: Mass Incarceration in the Age of Colorblindness*
Gordon Allport's *The Nature of Prejudice*
Albert Bandura's *Aggression: A Social Learning Analysis*
Hanna Batatu's *The Old Social Classes And The Revolutionary Movements Of Iraq*
Ha-Joon Chang's *Kicking Away the Ladder*
W. E. B. Du Bois's *The Souls of Black Folk*
Émile Durkheim's *On Suicide*
Frantz Fanon's *Black Skin, White Masks*
Frantz Fanon's *The Wretched of the Earth*
Eric Foner's *Reconstruction: America's Unfinished Revolution, 1863-1877*
Eugene Genovese's *Roll, Jordan, Roll: The World the Slaves Made*
Jack Goldstone's *Revolution and Rebellion in the Early Modern World*
Antonio Gramsci's *The Prison Notebooks*
Richard Herrnstein & Charles A Murray's *The Bell Curve: Intelligence and Class Structure in American Life*
Eric Hoffer's *The True Believer: Thoughts on the Nature of Mass Movements*
Jane Jacobs's *The Death and Life of Great American Cities*
Robert Lucas's *Why Doesn't Capital Flow from Rich to Poor Countries?*
Jay Macleod's *Ain't No Makin' It: Aspirations and Attainment in a Low Income Neighborhood*
Elaine May's *Homeward Bound: American Families in the Cold War Era*
Douglas McGregor's *The Human Side of Enterprise*
C. Wright Mills's *The Sociological Imagination*

Thomas Piketty's *Capital in the Twenty-First Century*
Robert D. Putman's *Bowling Alone*
David Riesman's *The Lonely Crowd: A Study of the Changing American Character*
Edward Said's *Orientalism*
Joan Wallach Scott's *Gender and the Politics of History*
Theda Skocpol's *States and Social Revolutions*
Max Weber's *The Protestant Ethic and the Spirit of Capitalism*

THEOLOGY

Augustine's *Confessions*
Benedict's *Rule of St Benedict*
Gustavo Gutiérrez's *A Theology of Liberation*
Carole Hillenbrand's *The Crusades: Islamic Perspectives*
David Hume's *Dialogues Concerning Natural Religion*
Immanuel Kant's *Religion within the Boundaries of Mere Reason*
Ernst Kantorowicz's *The King's Two Bodies: A Study in Medieval Political Theology*
Søren Kierkegaard's *The Sickness Unto Death*
C. S. Lewis's *The Abolition of Man*
Saba Mahmood's *The Politics of Piety: The Islamic Revival and the Feminist Subject*
Baruch Spinoza's *Ethics*
Keith Thomas's *Religion and the Decline of Magic*

COMING SOON

Chris Argyris's *The Individual and the Organisation*
Seyla Benhabib's *The Rights of Others*
Walter Benjamin's *The Work Of Art in the Age of Mechanical Reproduction*
John Berger's *Ways of Seeing*
Pierre Bourdieu's *Outline of a Theory of Practice*
Mary Douglas's *Purity and Danger*
Roland Dworkin's *Taking Rights Seriously*
James G. March's *Exploration and Exploitation in Organisational Learning*
Ikujiro Nonaka's *A Dynamic Theory of Organizational Knowledge Creation*
Griselda Pollock's *Vision and Difference*
Amartya Sen's *Inequality Re-Examined*
Susan Sontag's *On Photography*
Yasser Tabbaa's *The Transformation of Islamic Art*
Ludwig von Mises's *Theory of Money and Credit*

Macat Disciplines

*Access the greatest ideas and thinkers
across entire disciplines, including*

Postcolonial Studies

Roland Barthes's *Mythologies*
Frantz Fanon's *Black Skin, White Masks*
Homi K. Bhabha's *The Location of Culture*
Gustavo Gutiérrez's *A Theology of Liberation*
Edward Said's *Orientalism*
Gayatri Chakravorty Spivak's *Can the Subaltern Speak?*

Macat analyses are available from all good bookshops and libraries.

Access hundreds of analyses through one, multimedia tool.
Join free for one month **library.macat.com**

Macat Disciplines

Access the greatest ideas and thinkers across entire disciplines, including

FEMINISM, GENDER AND QUEER STUDIES

Simone De Beauvoir's
The Second Sex

Michel Foucault's
History of Sexuality

Betty Friedan's
The Feminine Mystique

Saba Mahmood's
*The Politics of Piety:
The Islamic Revival and
the Feminist Subject*

Joan Wallach Scott's
*Gender and the
Politics of History*

Mary Wollstonecraft's
*A Vindication of the
Rights of Woman*

Virginia Woolf's
A Room of One's Own

Judith Butler's
Gender Trouble

Macat analyses are available from all good bookshops and libraries.

Access hundreds of analyses through one, multimedia tool.
Join free for one month **library.macat.com**

Macat Disciplines

Access the greatest ideas and thinkers across entire disciplines, including

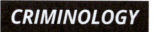

Macat Disciplines

Access the greatest ideas and thinkers across entire disciplines, including

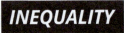

INEQUALITY

Ha-Joon Chang's, *Kicking Away the Ladder*

David Graeber's, *Debt: The First 5000 Years*

Robert E. Lucas's, *Why Doesn't Capital Flow from Rich To Poor Countries?*

Thomas Piketty's, *Capital in the Twenty-First Century*

Amartya Sen's, *Inequality Re-Examined*

Mahbub Ul Haq's, *Reflections on Human Development*

Macat analyses are available from all good bookshops and libraries.

Access hundreds of analyses through one, multimedia tool.
Join free for one month **library.macat.com**

Macat Disciplines

Access the greatest ideas and thinkers across entire disciplines, including

GLOBALIZATION

Arjun Appadurai's, *Modernity at Large: Cultural Dimensions of Globalisation*

James Ferguson's, *The Anti-Politics Machine*

Geert Hofstede's, *Culture's Consequences*

Amartya Sen's, *Development as Freedom*

Macat Pairs

Analyse historical and modern issues from opposite sides of an argument. Pairs include:

RACE AND IDENTITY

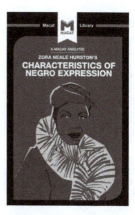

Zora Neale Hurston's
Characteristics of Negro Expression

Using material collected on anthropological expeditions to the South, Zora Neale Hurston explains how expression in African American culture in the early twentieth century departs from the art of white America. At the time, African American art was often criticized for copying white culture. For Hurston, this criticism misunderstood how art works. European tradition views art as something fixed. But Hurston describes a creative process that is alive, ever-changing, and largely improvisational. She maintains that African American art works through a process called 'mimicry'—where an imitated object or verbal pattern, for example, is reshaped and altered until it becomes something new, novel—and worthy of attention.

Frantz Fanon's
Black Skin, White Masks

Black Skin, White Masks offers a radical analysis of the psychological effects of colonization on the colonized.

Fanon witnessed the effects of colonization first hand both in his birthplace, Martinique, and again later in life when he worked as a psychiatrist in another French colony, Algeria. His text is uncompromising in form and argument. He dissects the dehumanizing effects of colonialism, arguing that it destroys the native sense of identity, forcing people to adapt to an alien set of values—including a core belief that they are inferior. This results in deep psychological trauma.

Fanon's work played a pivotal role in the civil rights movements of the 1960s.

Macat Pairs

Analyse historical and modern issues from opposite sides of an argument. Pairs include:

INTERNATIONAL RELATIONS IN THE 21ST CENTURY

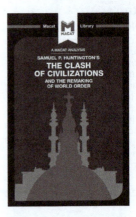

Samuel P. Huntington's
The Clash of Civilisations

In his highly influential 1996 book, Huntington offers a vision of a post-Cold War world in which conflict takes place not between competing ideologies but between cultures. The worst clash, he argues, will be between the Islamic world and the West: the West's arrogance and belief that its culture is a "gift" to the world will come into conflict with Islam's obstinacy and concern that its culture is under attack from a morally decadent "other."

Clash inspired much debate between different political schools of thought. But its greatest impact came in helping define American foreign policy in the wake of the 2001 terrorist attacks in New York and Washington.

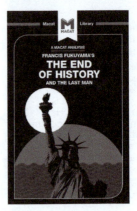

Francis Fukuyama's
The End of History and the Last Man

Published in 1992, *The End of History and the Last Man* argues that capitalist democracy is the final destination for all societies. Fukuyama believed democracy triumphed during the Cold War because it lacks the "fundamental contradictions" inherent in communism and satisfies our yearning for freedom and equality. Democracy therefore marks the endpoint in the evolution of ideology, and so the "end of history." There will still be "events," but no fundamental change in ideology.

Macat analyses are available from all good bookshops and libraries.

Access hundreds of analyses through one, multimedia tool.
Join free for one month **library.macat.com**

Macat Pairs

Analyse historical and modern issues from opposite sides of an argument. Pairs include:

HOW TO RUN AN ECONOMY

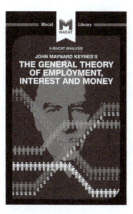

John Maynard Keynes's
The General Theory OF Employment, Interest and Money

Classical economics suggests that market economies are self-correcting in times of recession or depression, and tend toward full employment and output. But English economist John Maynard Keynes disagrees.

In his ground-breaking 1936 study *The General Theory*, Keynes argues that traditional economics has misunderstood the causes of unemployment. Employment is not determined by the price of labor; it is directly linked to demand. Keynes believes market economies are by nature unstable, and so require government intervention. Spurred on by the social catastrophe of the Great Depression of the 1930s, he sets out to revolutionize the way the world thinks

Milton Friedman's
The Role of Monetary Policy

Friedman's 1968 paper changed the course of economic theory. In just 17 pages, he demolished existing theory and outlined an effective alternate monetary policy designed to secure 'high employment, stable prices and rapid growth.'

Friedman demonstrated that monetary policy plays a vital role in broader economic stability and argued that economists got their monetary policy wrong in the 1950s and 1960s by misunderstanding the relationship between inflation and unemployment. Previous generations of economists had believed that governments could permanently decrease unemployment by permitting inflation—and vice versa. Friedman's most original contribution was to show that this supposed trade-off is an illusion that only works in the short term.

Macat analyses are available from all good bookshops and libraries.

Access hundreds of analyses through one, multimedia tool.
Join free for one month **library.macat.com**

Macat Pairs

Analyse historical and modern issues from opposite sides of an argument. Pairs include:

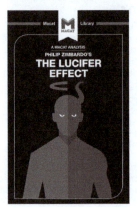

Macat Pairs

Analyse historical and modern issues from opposite sides of an argument. Pairs include:

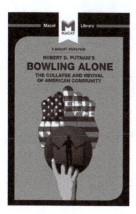